AS SEEN BY ME

LILIAN BELL

As Seen By Me

Lilian Bell

© 1st World Library, 2007
PO Box 2211
Fairfield, IA 52556
www.1stworldlibrary.com
First Edition

LCCN: 2007927806

Softcover ISBN: 978-1-4218-4554-8
Hardcover ISBN: 978-1-4218-4470-1
eBook ISBN: 978-1-4218-4638-5

Purchase *"As Seen By Me"*
as a traditional bound book at:
www.1stWorldLibrary.com/purchase.asp?ISBN=978-1-4218-4554-8

1st World Library is a literary, educational organization
dedicated to:

- Creating a free internet library of downloadable ebooks

- Hosting writing competitions and offering book publishing
  scholarships.

Interested in more 1st World Library books? contact:
literacy@1stworldlibrary.com
Check us out at: www.1stworldlibrary.com

1ˢᵗ World Library Literary Society

Giving Back to the World

"If you want to work on the core problem, it's early school literacy."

- James Barksdale, former CEO of Netscape

"No skill is more crucial to the future of a child, or to a democratic and prosperous society, than literacy."

- Los Angeles Times

"Literacy... means far more than learning how to read and write... The aim is to transmit... knowledge and promote social participation."

- UNESCO

"Literacy is not a luxury, it is a right and a responsibility. If our world is to meet the challenges of the twenty-first century we must harness the energy and creativity of all our citizens."

- President Bill Clinton

"Parents should be encouraged to read to their children, and teachers should be equipped with all available techniques for teaching literacy, so the varying needs and capacities of individual kids can be taken into account."

- Hugh Mackay

TO

THAT MOST INTERESTING SPECK OF HUMANITY,
ALL PERPETUAL MOTION AND
KINDLING INTELLIGENCE AND SWEETNESS
UNSPEAKABLE, MY LITTLE NEPHEW BILLY
ABSENCE FROM WHOM RACKED MY SPIRIT WITH
ITS MOST UNAPPEASABLE PANGS OF
HOMESICKNESS, AND WHOSE CONSTANT
PRESENCE IN MY STUDY SINCE MY RETURN HAS
SPARED THE PUBLIC NO SMALL AMOUNT OF PAIN

AUTHOR'S APOLOGY

The frank conceit of the title to this book will, I hope, not prejudice my friends against it, and will serve not only to excuse my being my own Boswell, but will fasten the blame of all inaccuracies, if such there be, upon the offender-- myself. This is not a continuous narrative of a continuous journey, but covers two years of travel over some thirty thousand miles, and presents peoples and things, not as you saw them, perhaps, or as they really are, but only As Seen By Me.

CONTENTS

I

FIRST LETTER—ON THE WAY

In this day and generation, when everybody goes to Europe, it is difficult to discover the only person who never has been there. But I am that one, and therefore the stir it occasioned in the bosom of my amiable family when I announced that I, too, was about to join the vast majority, is not easy to imagine. But if you think that I at once became a person of importance it only goes to show that you do not know the family. My mother, to be sure, hovered around me the way she does when she thinks I am going into typhoid fever. I never have had typhoid fever, but she is always on the watch for it, and if it ever comes it will not catch her napping. She will meet it half-way. And lest it elude her watchfulness, she minutely questions every pain which assails any one of us, for fear, it may be her dreaded foe. Yet when my sister's blessed lamb baby had it before he was a year old, and after he had got well and I was not afraid he would be struck dead for my wickedness, I said to her, "Well, mamma, you must have taken solid comfort out of the first real chance you ever had at your pet fever," she said I ought to be ashamed of myself.

My father began to explain international banking to me as his share in my preparations, but I utterly discouraged him by asking the difference between a check and a note. He said I reminded him of the juryman who asked the difference between plaintiff and defendant. I soothed him by assuring him that I knew I would always find somebody to go to the bank with me.

"Most likely 'twill be Providence, then, as He watches over children and fools," said my cousin, with what George Eliot calls "the brutal candor of a near relation."

My brother-in-law lent me ten Baedekers, and offered his hampers and French trunks to me with such reckless generosity that I had to get my sister to stop him so that I wouldn't hurt his feelings by refusing.

My sister said, "I am perfectly sure, mamma, that if I don't go with her, she will go about with an ecstatic smile on her face, and let herself get cheated and lost, and she would just as soon as not tell everybody that she had never been abroad before. She has no pride."

"Then you had better come along and take care of me and see that I don't disgrace you," I urged.

"Really, mamma, I do think I had better go," said my sister. So she actually consented to leave husband and baby in order to go and take care of me. I do assure you, however, that I have bought all the tickets, and carried the common purse, and got her through the custom-houses, and arranged prices thus far. But she does pack my trunks and make out the laundry lists—I will say that for her.

My brother's contribution to my comfort was in this wise: He said, "You must have a few more lessons on your wheel before you go, and I'll take you out for a lesson to-morrow if you'll get up and go at six o'clock in the morning—that is, if you'll wear gloves. But you mortify me half to death riding without gloves."

"Nobody sees me but milkmen," I said, humbly.

"Well, what will the milkmen think?" said my brother.

"Mercy on us, I never thought of that," I said. "My gloves are all pretty tight when one has to grip one's handle-bars as fiercely as I do. But I'll get large ones. What tint do you think milkmen care the most for?"

He sniffed.

"Well, I'll go and I'll wear gloves," I said, "but if I fall off, remember it will be on account of the gloves."

"You always do fall off," he said, with patient resignation. "I've seen you fall off that wheel in more different directions than it has spokes."

"I don't exactly fall," I explained, carefully. "I feel myself going and then I get off."

I was ready at six the next morning, and I wore gloves.

"Now, don't ride into the holes in the street"—one is obliged to give such instructions in Chicago—"and don't look at anything you see. Don't be afraid. You're all right. Now, then! You're off!"

"Oh, Teddy, don't ride so close to me," I quavered.

"I'm forty feet away from you," he said.

"Then double it," I said. "You're choking me by your proximity."

"Let's cross the railroad tracks just for practice," he said, when it was too late for me to expostulate. "Stand up on your pedals and ride fast, and—"

"Hold on, please do," I shrieked. "I'm falling off. Get out of my way. I seem to be turning—"

He scorched ahead, and I headed straight for the switchman's hut, rounded it neatly, and leaned myself and my wheel against the side of it, helpless with laughter.

A red Irish face, with a short black pipe in its mouth, thrust itself out of the tiny window just in front of me, and a voice with a rich brogue exclaimed:

"As purty a bit of riding as iver Oi see!"

"Wasn't it?" I cried. "You couldn't do it."

"Oi wouldn't thry! Oi'd rather tackle a railroad train going at full spheed thin wan av thim runaway critturs."

"Get down from there," hissed my brother so close to my ear that it made me bite my tongue.

I obediently scrambled down. Ted's face was very red.

"You ought to be ashamed of yourself to enter into immediate conversation with a man like that. What do you suppose that man thought of you?"

"Oh, perhaps he saw my gloves and took me for a lady," I pleaded.

Ted grinned and assisted me to mount.

When I successfully turned the corner by making Ted fall back out of sight, we rode away along the boulevard in silence for a while, for my conversation when I am on a wheel is generally limited to shrieks, ejaculations, and snatches of prayer. I never talk to be amusing.

"I say," said my brother, hesitatingly, "I wear a No. 8 glove and a No. 10 stocking."

"I've always thought you had large hands and feet," I said, ignoring the hint.

He giggled.

"No, now, really. I wish you'd write that down somewhere. You can get those things so cheap in Paris."

"You are supposing the case of my return, or of Christmas intervening, or—a present of some kind, I suppose."

"Well, no; not exactly. Although you know I am always broke—"

"Don't I, though?"

"And that I am still in debt—"

"Because papa insists upon your putting some money in the bank every month—"

"Yes, and the result is that I never get my head above water. I owe you twenty now."

"Which I never expect to recover, because you know I

always get silly about Christmas and 'forgive thee thy debts.'"

"You're awful good—" he began.

"But I'll be better if I bring you gloves and silk stockings."

"I'll give you the money!" he said, heroically. "Will you borrow it of me or of mamma?" I asked, with a chuckle at the family financiering which always goes on in this manner.

"Now don't make fun of me! *You* don't know what it is to be hard up."

"Don't I, though?" I said, indignantly. "Oh—oh! Catch me!"

He seized my handle-bar and righted me before I fell off.

"See what you did by saying I never was hard up," I said. "I'll tell you what, Teddy. You needn't give me the money. I'll bring you some gloves and stockings!"

"Oh, I say, honest? Oh, but you're the right kind of a sister! I'll never forget that as long as I live. You do look so nice on your wheel. You sit so straight and—"

I saw a milkman coming. We three were the only objects in sight, yet I headed for him.

"Get out of my way," I shrieked at him. "I'm a beginner. Turn off!"

He lashed his horse and cut down a side street.

"What a narrow escape," I sighed. "How glad I am I happened to think of that."

Lilian Bell

I looked up pleasantly at Ted. He was biting his lips and he looked raging.

"You are the most hopeless girl I ever saw!" he burst out. "I wish you didn't own a wheel."

"I don't," I said. "The wheel owns me."

"You haven't the manners of—"

"Stockings," I said, looking straight ahead. "Silk stockings with polka dots embroidered on them, No. 10."

Ted looked sheepish.

"I ride so well," I proceeded. "I sit up so straight and look so nice."

No answer.

"Gloves," I went on, still without looking at him. "White and pearl ones for evening, and russet gloves for the street, No. 8."

"Oh, quit, won't you? I'm sorry I said that. But if you only knew how you mortify me."

"Cheer up, Tedcastle. I am going away, you know. And when I come back you will either have got over caring so much or I will be more of a lady."

"I'm sorry you are going," said my brother. "But as you are going, perhaps you will let me use your rooms while you are gone. Your bed is the best one I ever slept in, and your study would be bully for the boys when they come to see me."

I was too stunned to reply. He went on, utterly oblivious of my consternation:

"And I am going to use your wheel while you are gone, if you don't mind, to take the girls out on. I know some awfully nice girls who can ride, but their wheels are last year's make, and they won't ride them. I'd rather like to be able to offer them a new wheel."

"I am not going to take all my party dresses. Have you any use for them?" I said.

"Why, what's the matter? Won't you let me have your rooms?"

"Merciful heavens, child! I should say not!"

"Why, I haven't asked you for much," said my small, modest brother. "You offered."

"Well, just wait till I offer the rest. But I'll tell you what I will do, Ted. If you will promise not to go into my rooms and rummage once while I am gone, and not to touch my wheel, I'll buy you a tandem, and then you can take the girls on that."

"I'd rather have you bring me some things from Europe," said my shrinking brother.

"All right. I'll do that, but let me off this thing. I am so tired I can't move. You'll have to walk it back and give me five cents to ride home on the car."

I crawled in to breakfast more dead than alive.

"What's the matter, dearie? Did you ride too far?"

Lilian Bell

asked mamma.

"I don't know whether I rode too far or whether it was Ted's asking if he couldn't use my rooms while I was gone, but something has made me tired. What's that? Whom is papa talking to over the telephone?"

Papa came in fuming and fretting.

"Who was it this time?" I questioned, with anticipation. Inquiries over the telephone were sure to be interesting to me just now.

"Somebody who wanted to know what train you were going on, but would not give his name. He was inquiring for a friend, he said, and wouldn't give his friend's name either."

"Didn't you tell him?" I cried, in distress.

"Certainly not. I told him nobody but an idiot would withhold his name."

Papa calls such a variety of men idiots.

"Oh, but it was probably only flowers or candy. Why didn't you tell him? Have you no sentiment?"

"I won't have you receiving anonymous communications," he retorted, with the liberty fathers have a little way of taking with their daughters.

"But flowers," I pleaded. "It is no harm to send flowers without a card. Don't you see?" Oh, how hard it is to explain a delicate point like that to one's father—in broad daylight! "I am supposed to know who sent them!"

"But would you know?" asked my practical ancestor.

"Not—not exactly. But it would be almost sure to be one of them."

Ted shouted. But there was nothing funny in what I said. Boys are so silly.

"Anyway, I am sorry you didn't tell him," I said.

"Well, I'm not," declared papa.

The rest of the day fairly flew. The last night came, and the baby was put to bed. I undressed him, which he regarded as such a joke that he worked himself into a fever of excitement. He loves to scrub like Josie, the cook. I had bought him a little red pail, and I gave it to him that night when he was partly undressed, and he was so enchanted with it that he scampered around hugging it, and saying, "Pile! pile!" like a little Cockney. He gave such squeals of ecstasy that everybody came into the nursery to find him scrubbing his crib with a nail-brush and little red pail.

"Who gave you the pretty pail, Billy?" asked Aunt Lida, who was sitting by the crib.

"Tattah," said Billy, in a whisper. He always whispers my name.

"Then go and kiss dear auntie. She is going away on the big boat to stay such a long time."

Billy's face sobered. Then he dropped his precious pail, and came and licked my face like a little dog, which is his way of kissing.

I squeezed him until he yelled.

"Don't let him forget me," I wailed. "Talk to him about me every day. And buy him a toy out of my money often, and tell him Tattah sent it to him. Oh, oh, he'll be grown up when I come home!"

"Don't cry, dearie," said Aunt Lida, handing me her handkerchief. "I'll see that your grave is kept green."

My sister appeared at the door. She was all ready to start. She even had her veil on.

"What do you mean by exciting Billy so at this time of night?" she said. "Go out, all of you. We'll lose the train. Hush, somebody's at the telephone. Papa's talking to that same man again." I jumped up and ran out.

"Let me answer it, papa dear! Yes, yes, yes, certainly. To-night on the Pennsylvania. You're quite welcome. Not at all." I hung up the telephone.

I could hear papa in the nursery:

"She actually told him—after all I said this morning! I never heard of anything like it."

Two or three voices were raised in my defence. Ted slipped out into the hall.

"Bully for you," he whispered. "You'll get the flowers all right at the train. Who do you s'pose they're from? Another box just came for you. Say, couldn't you leave that smallest box of violets in the silver box? I want to give them to a girl, and you've got such loads of others."

"Don't ask her for those," answered my dear sister, "they are the most precious of all!"

"I can't give you any of mine," I said, "but I'll buy you a box for her—a small box," I added hastily.

"The carriages have come, dears," quavered grandmamma, coming out of the nursery, followed by the family, one after the other.

"Get her satchels, Teddy. Her hat is upstairs. Her flowers are in the hall. She left her ulster on my bed, and her books are on the window-sill," said mamma. She wouldn't look at me. "Remember, dearie, your medicines are all labelled, and I put needles in your work-box all threaded. Don't sit in draughts and don't read in a dim light. Have a good time and study hard and come back soon. Good—bye, my girlie. God bless you!"

By this time no handkerchief would have sufficed for my tears. I reached out blindly, and Ted handed me a towel.

"I've got a sheet when you've sopped that," he said. Boys are such brutes.

Aunt Lida said, "Good-bye, my dearest. You are my favorite niece. You know I love you the best."

I giggled, for she tells my sister the same thing always.

"Nobody seems to care much that I am going," said Bee, mournfully.

"But you are coming back so soon, and she is going to stay so long," exclaimed grandmamma, patting Bee.

Lilian Bell

"I'll bet she doesn't stay a year," cried Ted.

"I'll expect her home by Christmas," said papa.

"I'll bet she is here to eat Thanksgiving dinner," cried my brother-in-law.

"No, she is sure to stay as long as she has said she would," said mamma.

Mothers are the brace of the universe. The family trailed down to the front door. Everybody was carrying something. There were two carriages, for they were all going to the station with us.

"For all the world like a funeral, with loads of flowers and everybody crying," said my brother, cheerfully.

I never shall forget that drive to the station; nor the last few moments, when Bee and I stood on the car-steps and talked to those who were on the platform of the station. Can anybody else remember how she felt at going to Europe for the first time and leaving everybody she loved at home? Bee grieved because there were no flowers at the train after all. But the next morning they appeared, a tremendous box, arranged as a surprise.

Telegrams came popping in at all the big stations along the way, enlivening our gloom, and at the steamer there were such loads of things that we might almost have set up as a florist, or fruiterer, or bookseller. Such a lapful of steamer letters and telegrams! I read a few each morning, and some of them I read every morning!

I don't like ocean travel. They sent grapefruit and confections to my state-room, which I tossed out of the port-hole. You know there are some people who think you don't know what you want. I travelled horizontally most of the way, and now people roar when I say I wasn't ill. Well, I wasn't, you know. We—well, Teddy would not like me to be more explicit. I own to a horrible headache which never left me. I deny everything else. Let them laugh. I was there, and I know.

The steamer I went on allows men to smoke on all the decks, and they all smoked in my face. It did not help me. I must say that I was unspeakably thankful to get my foot on dry ground once more. When we got to the dock a special train of toy cars took us through the greenest of green landscapes, and suddenly, almost before we knew it, we were at Waterloo Station, and knew that London was at our door.

Lilian Bell

II

LONDON

People said to me, "What are you going to London for?" I said, "To get an English point of view." "Very well," said one of the knowing ones, who has lived abroad the larger part of his life, "then you must go to 'The Insular,' in Piccadilly. That is not only the smartest hotel in London, but it is the most typically British. The rooms are let from season to season to the best country families. There you will find yourself plunged headlong into English life with not an American environment to bless yourself with, and you will soon get your English point of view."

"Ah-h," responded the simpleton who goes by my name, "that is what we want. We will go to 'The Insular.'"

We wrote at once for rooms, and then telegraphed for them from Southampton.

The steamer did not land her passengers until the morning of the ninth day, which shows the vast superiority of going on a fast boat, which gets you in fully as much as fifteen or twenty minutes ahead of the slow ones.

Our luggage would not go on even a four-wheeler, so we

took a dear little private bus and proceeded to put our mountainous American trunks on it. We filled the top of this bus as full as it would hold, and put everything else inside. After stowing ourselves in there would not have been room even for another umbrella.

In this fashion we reached "The Insular," where we were received by four or five gorgeous creatures in livery, the head one of whom said, "Miss Columbia?" I admitted it, and we were ushered in, where we were met by more belonging to this tribe of gorgeousness, another of whom said, "Miss Columbia?"

"Yes," I said, firmly, privately wondering if they were trying to trip me into admitting that I was somebody else.

"The housekeeper will be here presently," said this person. "She is expecting you."

Forth came the housekeeper.

"Miss Columbia?" she said.

Once again I said "Yes," patiently, standing on my other foot.

"If you will be good enough to come with me I will show you your rooms."

A door opened outward, disclosing a little square place with two cane-bottomed chairs. A man bounced out so suddenly that I nearly annihilated my sister, who was back of me. I could not imagine what this little cubbyhole was, but as there seemed to be nowhere else to go, I went in. The others followed, then the man who had bounced out. He closed the door and shut us in, where we stood in solemn silence. About a quarter of an hour afterwards I thought I saw something through the glass moving slowly downward, and then an infinitesimal thrill in the soles of my feet led me to suspect the truth.

"Is this thing an elevator?" I whispered to my sister.

"No, they call it a lift over here," she whispered back.

"I know that," I murmured, impatiently. "But is this thing it? Are we moving? Are we going anywhere?"

"Why, of course, my dear. They are slower than ours, that's all."

I listened to her with some misgivings, for her information is not always to be wholly trusted, but this time it happened that she was right, for after a while we came to the fourth floor, where our rooms were.

I wish you could have seen the size of them. I shall not attempt to describe them, for you would not believe me. I had engaged "two rooms and a bath." The two rooms were there. "Where is the bath?" I said. The housekeeper lovingly, removed a gigantic crash towel from a hideous tin object, and proudly exposed to my vision that object which is next dearest to his silk hat to an Englishman's heart—a hip-bath tub. Her manner said, "Beat that if you can."

My sister prodded me in the back with her umbrella, which in our sign language means, "Don't make a scene."

"Very well," I said, rather meekly. "Have our trunks sent up."

"Very good, madam."

She went away, and then we rang the bell and began to order what were to us the barest necessities of life. We were tired and lame and sleepy from a night spent at the pier landing the luggage, and we wanted things with which to make ourselves comfortable.

There was a pocket edition of a fireplace, and they brought us a hatful of the vilest soft coal, which peppered everything in the rooms with soot.

We climbed over our trunks to sit by this imitation of a fire, only to find that there was nothing to sit on but the most uncompromising of straight-backed chairs.

We groaned as we took in the situation. To our poor, racked frames a coal-hod would not have suggested more discomfort. We dragged up our hampers, packed with steamer-rugs and pillows, and my sister sat on hers while I took another turn at the bell. While the maid is answering this bell I shall have plenty of time to tell you what we afterwards discovered the process of bell-ringing in an English hotel to be.

We rang our bell. Presently we heard the most horrible gong, such as we use on our patrol wagons and fire-engines at home. This clanged four times. Then a second bell down the hall answered it. Then feet flew by our door. At this juncture my sister and I prepared to let ourselves down the fire-escape. But we soon discovered that those flying feet belonged to the poor maid, whom that gong had signalled that she was wanted on the fourth floor. She flew to a speaking-tube and asked who on the fourth floor wanted her. She was then given the number of our room, when she rang a bell to signify that our call was answered, by which time she was at liberty, and knocked at our door, saying, in her soft English voice, "Did you ring, miss?"

We told her we wanted rocking-chairs. She said there was not one in the house. Then easy-chairs, we said, or anything cushioned or low or comfortable. She said the housekeeper had no easier chairs.

We sat down on our hampers, and my sister leaned against the corner of the wardrobe with a pillow at her back to keep from being cut in two. I propped my back against the wash-stand, which did very well, except that the wash-stand occasionally slid away from me.

"This," said my sister, impressively, "is England."

We had been here only half an hour, but I had already got my point of view.

"Let's go out and look up a hotel where they take Americans," I said. "I feel the need of ice-water."

Our drinking-water at "The Insular" was on the end of the wash-stand nearest the fire.

So, feeling a little timid and nervous, but not in the least homesick, we went downstairs. One of our gorgeous retinue called a cab and we entered it.

"Where shall we go?" asked my sister.

"I feel like saying to the first hotel we see," I said.

Just then we raised our eyes and they rested simultaneously upon a sign, "The Empire Hotel for Cats and Dogs." This simple solution of our difficulty put us in such high good humor that we said we wouldn't look up a hotel just yet—we would take a drive.

Under these circumstances we took our first drive down Piccadilly, and Europe to me dates from that moment. The ship, the landing, the custom-house, the train, the hotel—all these were mere preliminaries to the Europe, which began then. People told me in America how my heart would swell at this, and how I would thrill at that, but it was not so. My first real thrill came to me in Piccadilly. It went all over me in little shivers and came out at the ends of my fingers, and then began once more at the base of my brain and did it all over again.

But what is the use of describing one's first view of London streets and traffic to the initiated? Can they, who became used to it as children, appreciate it? Can they look back and recall how it struck them? No. When I try to tell Americans over here they look at me curiously and say, "Dear me, how odd!" The way they say it leaves me to draw any one of three conclusions: either they are not impressionable, and are therefore honest in denying the feeling; or they think it vulgar to admit it; or I am the only grown person in America who never has been to Europe before.

But I am indifferent to their opinion. People are right in saying this great tremendous rush of feeling can come but once. It is like being in love for the first time. You like it and yet you don't like it. You wish it would go away, yet you fear that it will go all too soon. It gets into your head and makes you dizzy, and you want to shut your eyes, but you are afraid if you do that you will miss something. You cannot eat and you cannot sleep, and you feel that you have two consciousnesses: one which belongs to the life you have lived hitherto, and which still is going on, somewhere in the world, unmindful of you, and you unmindful of it; and the other is this new bliss which is beating in your veins and sounding in your ears and shining before your eyes, which no one knows and no one dreams of, but which keeps a smile on your lips—a smile which has in it nothing of humor, nothing from the great without, but which-comes from the secret recesses of your own inner consciousness, where the heart of the matter lies.

I remember nothing definite about that first drive. I, for my part, saw with unseeing eyes. My sister had seen it all before, so she had the power of speech. Occasionally she prodded me and cried, "Look, oh! look quickly." But I never swerved. "I can't look. If I do I shall miss something. You attend to your own window and I'll attend to mine. Coming back I will see your side."

When we got beyond the shops I said to the cabman:

"Do you know exactly the way you have come?"

"Yes, miss," he said.

"Then go back precisely the same way."

"Have you lost something, miss?" he inquired.

"Yes," I said, "I have lost an impression, and I must look till I find it."

"Very good, miss," he said.

If I had said, "I have carelessly let fall my cathedral," or, "I have lost my orang-outang. Look for him!" an imperturbable British cabby would only touch his cap and say, "Very good, miss!"

So we followed our own trail back to "The Insular." "In this way," I said to my sister, "we both get a complete view. To-morrow we will do it all over again."

But we found that we could not wait for the morrow. We did it all over again that afternoon, and that second time I was able in a measure to detach myself from the hum and buzz and the dizzying effect of foreign faces, and I began to locate impressions. My first distinct recollections are of the great numbers of high hats on the men, the ill-hanging skirts and big feet of the women, the unsteadying effect of all those thousands of cabs, carriages, and carts all going to the left, which kept me constantly wishing to shriek out, "Go to the right or we'll all be killed," the absolutely perfect manner in which traffic was managed, and the majestic authority of the London police.

I have seen the Houses of Parliament and the Tower and Westminster Abbey, and the World's Fair, but the most impressive sight I ever beheld is the upraised hand of a London policeman. I never heard one of them speak except when spoken to. But let one little blue-coated man raise his forefinger and every vehicle on wheels stops, and stops instantly; stops in obedience to law and order; stops without swearing or gesticulating or abuse; stops with no under-handed trying to drive out of line and get by on the other side; just stops, that is the end of it. And why? Because the Queen of England is behind that raised finger. A London policeman has more power than our President.

Even the Queen's coachmen obey that forefinger. Not long ago she dismissed one who dared to drive even the royal carriage on in defiance of it. Understanding how to obey, that is what makes liberty.

I am the most flamboyant of Americans, the most hopelessly addicted to my own country, but I must admit that I had my first real taste of liberty in England.

I will tell you why. In America nobody obeys anybody. We

make our laws, and then most industriously set about studying out a plan by which we may evade them. America is suffering, as all republics must of necessity suffer, from liberty in the hands of the multitude. The multitude are ignorant, and liberty in the hands of the ignorant is always license.

In America, the land of the free, whom do we fear? The President? No, God bless him. There is not a true American in the world who would not stand up as a man or a woman and go into his presence without fear. Are we afraid of our Senators, our chief rulers? No. But we are afraid of our servants, of our street-car conductors. We are afraid of sleeping-car porters, and the drivers of huge trucks. We are afraid they will drive over us in the streets, and if we dare to assert our rights and hold them in check we are afraid of what they will say to us, in the name of liberty, and of the way they will look at us, in the name of liberty.

English servants, I have discovered, have no more respect for Americans than the old-time negro of the Southern aristocracy has for Northerners. I once asked an old black mammy in Georgia why the negroes had so little respect for the white ladies of the North. "Case dey don' know how to treat black folks, honey." "Why don't they?" I persisted. "Are they not kind to you?" "Umph," she responded (and no one who has never heard a fat old negress say "Umph" knows the eloquence of it). "Umph. Dat's it. Dey's too kin'. Dey don' know how to mek us min'." And that is just the trouble with Americans here. An English servant takes orders, not requests.

I had such a time to learn that. We could not understand why we were obeyed so well at first, and presently, without any outward disrespect, our wants were simply ignored until all the English people had been attended to.

My sister had told me I was too polite, but one never believes one's sister, so I questioned our sweet English friends, and they, with much delicacy and many apologies, and the prettiest hesitation in the world—considering the situation—told us the reason.

"But," I gasped, "if I should speak to our servants in that manner they would leave. They would not stay over night." Our English friends tried not to smile in a superior way, and they succeeded, only I knew the smile was there, and said, "Oh, no, our servants never leave us. They apologize for having done it wrong."

On the way home I plucked up courage. "I am going to try it," I said, firmly. My sister laughed in derision.

"Now I could do it," she said, complaisantly. And so she could. My sister never plumes herself on a quality she does not possess.

"Are you going to use the tone and everything?" I said, somewhat timidly.

"You wait and see."

She hesitated some time, I noticed, before she rang the bell, and she looked at herself in the glass and cleared her throat. I knew she was bracing herself.

"I'll ring the bell if you like," I said, politely.

She gave one look at me and then rang the bell herself with a firm hand.

"And I'll get behind you with a poker in One hand and a pitcher of hot water in the other. Speak when you need either."

"You feel very funny when you don't have to do it yourself," she said, witheringly.

"You'll never put it through. You'll back down and say 'please' before you have finished," I said, and just then the maid knocked at the door.

I never heard anything like it. My sister was superb. I doubt if Bernhardt at her best ever inspired me with more awe. How that maid flew around. How humble she was. How she apologized. And how, every time my sister said, "Look sharp, now," the maid said, "Thank you." I thought I should die. I was so much interested in the dramatic possibilities of my cherished sister that when the door closed behind the maid we simply looked at each other a moment, then simultaneously made a bound for the bed, where we choked with laughter among the pillows. Presently we sat up with flushed faces and rumpled hair. I reached over and shook hands with her.

"How was that?" she asked.

"'Twas grand," I said. "The Queen couldn't have done it more to the manner born."

My sister accepted my compliments complaisantly, as one who should say, "'Tis no more than my deserts."

"How firm you were," I said, admiringly.

"Wasn't I, though?"

"How humble she was."

"Wasn't she?"

"You were quite as disagreeable and determined as a real Englishwoman would have been."

"So I was."

A pause full of intense admiration on my part. Then she said, "You couldn't have done it."

"I know that."

"You are so deadly civil."

"Not to everybody, only to servants." I said this apologetically.

"You never keep a steady hand. You either grovel at their feet or snap their heads off."

"Quite true," I admitted, humbly.

"But it was grand, wasn't it?" she said.

"Unspeakably grand."

And for Americans it was.

We were still at "The Insular," when one day I took up a handful of what had once been a tight bodice, and said to my sister:

"See how thin I've grown! I believe I am starving to death."

"No wonder," she answered, gloomily, "with this awful English cooking! I'm nearly dead from your experiment of getting an English point of view. I want something to eat—something that I *like*. I want a beefsteak, with mushrooms, and some potatoes *au gratin*, like those we have in America. I hate the stuff we get here. I wish I could never see another chop as long as I live."

"'The Insular' is considered very good," I remarked, pensively.

"Considered!" cried she. "Whose consideration counts, I should like to know, when you are always hungry for something you can't get?"

"I know it; and we are paying such prices, too. Who, except ostriches, could eat their nasty preserves for breakfast when they are having grape-fruit at home? And then their vile aspic jellies and potted meats for luncheon, which look like sausage congealed in cold gravy, and which taste like gum arabic."

"Let's move," said my sister. "Not into another hotel—that wouldn't be much better. But lot's take lodgings. I've heard that they were lovely. Then we can order what we like. Besides, it will be very much cheaper."

"I didn't come over here to economize," I said.

"Well, I wouldn't say a word if we were getting anything for our money, but we are not. Besides, when you get to Paris you will wish you hadn't been so extravagant here."

"Are the Paris shops more fascinating than those in Regent Street?" I asked.

"Much more."

"More alluring, than Bond Street?"

"More so than any in the world," she affirmed, with the religious fervor which always characterizes her tone when she speaks of Paris. The very leather of her purse fairly squeaks with ecstasy when she thinks of Paris.

"Heavens!" I murmured, with awe, for whenever she won't go to Du Maurier's grave with me, and when I won't do the crown jewels in the Tower with her, we always compromise amiably on Bond Street, and come home beaming with joy.

"We might go now just to look," I said. "I have the addresses of some very good lodgings."

"We'll take a cab by the hour," said she, putting her hat on before the mirror, and turning her head on one side to view her completed handiwork.

"Now take off that watch and that belt and that chatelaine if you don't want these harpies to think we are 'rich Americans' (how I have come to hate that phrase over here!), because they will charge accordingly."

She looked at me with genuine admiration.

"Do you know, dear, you are really clever at times?"

I colored with pleasure. It is so seldom that she finds anything practical in me to praise.

"Now mind, we are just going to look," she cautioned, as we rang a bell. "We must not do anything in a hurry."

We came out half an hour afterwards and got into the cab without looking at each other.

"It was very unbusinesslike," said she, severely. "You never do anything right."

"But it was so gloriously impudent of us," I urged. "First, we wanted lodgings. This was a boarding-house. Second, we wanted two bed-rooms and a drawing-room. They had only one drawing-room in the house; could we have that? Yes, we could. So we took their whole first floor, and made them promise to serve our breakfasts in bed, and our other meals in their best drawing-room, and turned a boarding-house into a lodging-house, all inside of half an hour. It was lovely!"

"It was bad business," said she. "We could have got it for less, but you are always in such a hurry. If you like a thing, and anybody says you may have it for fifty, you always say, 'I'll give you seventy-five,' You're so afraid to think a thing over."

"Second thoughts are never as much fun as first thoughts," I urged. "Second thoughts are always so sensible and reasonable and approved of."

"How do you know?" asked my sister, witheringly. "You never waited for any."

The next day we moved. Everybody said our rooms were charming, and that they were cheap, for I told how much we paid, much to my sister's disgust. She is *such* a lady.

"We have cut down our expenses so much," I said, looking around on the drab walls and the dun-colored carpets, "don't you think we might have a few flowers?"

"I believe you took this place for the balcony, so that you could put daisies around the edge and in the window-boxes!" she cried.

"No, I didn't. But the houses in London are so pretty with their flowers. Don't you think we might have a few?"

"Well, go and get them. I've got to write the home letter to-day if it is to catch the Southampton boat."

I came home with six huge palms, two June roses, some pink heather, a jar of marguerites, and I had ordered the balcony and window-boxes filled. My sister helped me to place them, but when her back was turned I arranged them over again. I can't tie a veil on the way she can, but I can arrange flowers to look—well, I won't boast.

Our landladies were two middle-aged, comfortable sisters. We called them "The Tabbies," meaning no disrespect to cats, either. I thought they took rather too violent an interest in our affairs, but I said nothing until one day after we had been settled nearly a week. I was seated in my own private room trying to write. My sister came in, evidently disturbed by something.

"Do you know," she said, "that our landlady just asked me how much you paid for those strawberries? And when I told her she said that that made them come to fourpence apiece, and that they were very dear. Now, how did she know that they were strawberries, or how many were in each box, I'd like to know?"

"Probably she opened the package," I said.

"Exactly what I think. Now I won't stand that. And then she asked me not to set things on the mahogany tables. It's just because we are Americans! She never would dare treat English people that way. She has not sufficient respect for us."

"Then tell her to be more respectful; tell her we are very highly thought of at home."

"She wouldn't care for that."

"Then tell her we have a few rich relations and quite a number of influential friends."

"Pooh!"

"And if that does not fetch her, there is nothing left to do but to be quite rude to her, and then she will know that we belong to the very highest society. But what do you care what a middle-class landlady thinks, just so she lets you alone?"

My sister meditated, and I added:

"If you would just snub her once, in your most ladylike way, it would settle her. As for me, I am satisfied to think we are paying much less, and we are twice as comfortable as we were at the hotel; and we get such good things to eat that our skeletons are filling out, and once more our clothes fit."

"That is so," said she, letting her thoughts wander to the number of hooks in her closet. "We do have more room, and I think our drawing-room with its palms and flowers will look lovely to-morrow."

"Do you think it was wise," she added, "to ask all those men to come at once?"

"Oh yes; let them all come together, then we can weed them out afterwards. You never can have too many men."

"I am glad you have asked in a few women."

"Why?" I demanded. "Are you insinuating that we are not equal to a handful of Englishmen? Recall the Boston tea-party. We will give them the first strawberries of the season, and plenty of tea. Feed them; that's the main thing," I said, firmly, taking up my pen and looking steadily at her.

"I'll go," she said, hastily. "Do you have to go to the bank to-day? You know to-morrow we must pay our weekly bill."

"It won't be much," I said, cheerfully; "I am sure I have enough."

The next day the bill came. Our landlady sent it up on the breakfast-tray. I opened it, then shrieked for my sister. It covered four pages of note-paper.

"For heaven's sake! what is the matter?" she cried. "Has anything happened to Billy?"

"Billy! This thing is not an American letter. It is the bill for our cheap lodgings. Look at it! Look at the extras—gas, coals, washing bed—linen, washing table—linen, washing towels, kitchen fires, service, oil for three lamps, afternoon tea, and three shillings for sundries on the fourth page! What can sundries include? She hasn't skipped anything but pew-rent."

My sister looked at the total, and buried her face in the pillows to smother a groan.

"Ring the bell," I said; "I want the maid."

"What are you going to do?"

"I'm going to find out what 'sundries' are."

She gave the bell-cord such a pull that she broke the wire, and it fell down on her head.

"That, too, will go in the bill. Wrap your handkerchief around your hand and give the wire a jerk. Give it a good one. I don't care if it brings the police."

The maid came.

"Martha, present my compliments to Mrs. Black, and ask her what 'sundries' include."

Martha came back smiling.

"Please, miss, Mrs. Black's compliments, and 'sundries' means that you complained that the coffee was muddy, and after that she cleared it with an egg. 'Sundries' means the eggs."

"Martha," I said, weakly, "give me those Crown salts. No, no, I forgot; those are Mrs. Black's salts. Take them out and tell her I only smelled them once."

"Martha," said my sister, dragging my purse out from under my pillow, "here is sixpence not to tell Mrs. Black anything." Then when Martha disappeared she said, "How often have I told you not to jest with servants?"

"I forgot," I said, humbly. "But Martha has a sense of humor, don't you think?"

"I never thought anything about it. But what are you going to do about that bill?"

"I'm going to argue about it, and declare I won't pay it, and then pay it like a true American. Would you have me upset the traditions? But I've got to go to the bank first."

I did just as I said. I argued to no avail. Mrs. Black was quite haughty, and made me feel like a chimney-sweep. I paid her in full, and when I came up I said:

"You are quite right. She has a poor opinion of us. When I asked her how long it would take to drive to a house in West End, she said, 'Why do you want to know?' I said I 'wanted to see the house.'"

"Didn't you tell her we were *invited* there?" asked my sister, scandalized.

"No; I said I had heard a good deal about the house, and she said it was open to the public on Fridays. So I said we'd go then."

"I think you are horrid!" cried Bee. "The insolence of that woman! And you actually think it is funny! You think *everything* is funny."

I soothed her by pointing out some of the things which I considered sad, notably English people trying to enjoy themselves. Then the men began to drop in for tea, and that succeeded in making her forget her troubles.

Reggie and the Duke arrived together. My sister at once took charge of the Duke, while Reggie said to me, "I say, what sort of creature is the old girl below?"

"Not a very good sort, I am afraid. Why? What has she done now?"

"Why, she stopped Abingdon and me and asked us to wipe our shoes."

"She asked the Duke of Abingdon to wipe his shoes?" I gasped, in a whisper.

"Yes; and Freddie, who was just ahead of us, turned back and said, 'My good woman, was the cab very dirty, do you think?'"

"Oh, don't tell my sister! She has almost died of Mrs. Black already to-day; this would finish her completely."

"Well, you must give your woman a talking to—a regular going over, d'ye know? Tell her you'll be the mistress of the whole blooming house or you'll tear it to pieces. That's the way to talk to 'em. I told my landlady in Edinburgh once that I'd chuck her out of the window if she spoke to me until she was spoken to. She came up and rapped on the door one Saturday night at ten o'clock, when I had some fellows there, and told me to send those men home and go to bed."

"Then she isn't taking advantage of us because we are Americans, the way the cabmen do?"

"Oh yes, I dare say she is; but you must stand up to her. They're a set of thieves, the whole of 'em. I say, that's a pretty picture you've got pinned up there."

"That's to hide a hole in the lace curtain," I explained, gratuitously. Then I remembered, and glanced apprehensively at my sister, but fortunately she had not heard me. "That is one of the pictures from *Truth*, an American magazine. I always save the middle picture when it is pretty, and pin it up on the wall."

"That is one thing where the States are away ahead of us—in their illustrated magazines."

"Don't say 'the States!' I've told you before. I didn't know you ever admitted that anything was better in America."

Reggie only smiled affably. He ignored my offer of battle, and said:

"Abingdon is asking your sister to dine. I'm asked, and Freddie and his wife, and I think you will enjoy it."

When they were all gone I marched downstairs to Mrs. Black without saying a word to any one. When I came up I found my sister hanging over the banisters.

"What is the matter? What have you done? I knew you were angry by the way you looked."

"It was lovely!" I said. "I sent for Mrs. Black, and said, 'Mrs. Black, do you know the name of the gentleman whom you asked to wipe his shoes to-day?' 'No,' said she. 'It was the Duke of Abingdon,' I said, sternly, well knowing the unspeakable reverence which the middle-class English have for a title. She turned purple. She fell back against the wall, muttering, 'The Duke of Abingdon! The Duke of Abingdon!' I believe she is still leaning up against the wall muttering that holy name. A title to Mrs. Black!"

The next day both the Tabbies were curtsying in the hall when we started out. We were going on a coach to Richmond with Julia and her husband, and another American girl, and then Julia's husband was going to row us up the Thames to Hampton Court for tea, and they were all going to dine with us at Scott's when we got home.

It was a lovely day. The trees were a mass of bloom, and everybody ought to have enjoyed himself. We were having a very good time of it among ourselves reading the absurd signs, until we noticed the three girls who sat opposite to us. They had serious faces, and long, consumptive teeth, which they never succeeded in completely hiding. I knew just how they would look when they were dead; I knew that those two long front teeth would still— They listened to all we said without a flicker of the eyelashes. Occasionally they looked down at the size of the American girl's little feet and then involuntarily drew their own back out of sight.

Presently I espied a sign, "Funerals, for this week only, at half price." I seized Julia's hand. "Stop, oh, stop the coach and let's get a funeral! We may never have an opportunity to get a bargain in funerals again. And the sale lasts only one week. Everybody told me before I came away to get what I wanted at the moment I saw it; not to wait, thinking I would come back. So unless we order one now we may have to pay the full price. And a funeral would be such a good investment; it would keep forever. You'd never feel like using it before you actually needed it. Do let me get one now!"

Of course, Julia, my sister, and Julia's husband were in gales of laughter; but what finished me off was to see three serious creatures opposite rise as if pulled by one string, look in an anxious way at me and then at the sign, while the teeth began to say to each other: "What did she say? What does she mean? What does she want a funeral for?"

We had a lovely day, but everybody we met on the river looked very unhappy, and nobody seemed to be at all glad that we were there or that we were rising to the occasion. When we got home I was too tired to notice things, but my sister, who sees everything, whispered:

"I verily believe they've put down a new stair-carpet to-day."

The next morning such a sight met our astonished eyes. There was a new carpet on the hall. There were new curtains in our drawing-room. All the covers had been removed from their sacred furniture. Brass andirons replaced the old ones. The piano had a new cover. There was a rocking-chair for each (we had only one before), and while we were still speechless with amazement Mrs. Black came in with our bill.

"I have been thinking this over since yesterday, and I have decided that as long as you did not understand about the extras, it would be no more than right that I should take them off. So I owe you this."

I took the money, and it dropped from my nerveless fingers. Mrs. Black picked it up and put it on the table—the mahogany table.

"You see I propped your palms for you in your absence, and I repotted four of them. I thought they would grow better. Here are some periodicals I sent to the library for, thinking you might like to look at them, and I put my new calendar over your writing-desk. Now, is there any little delicacy you would like for your luncheon?"

While Bee was getting rid of her I made a few rapid mental calculations.

"Bee," I said, "we are going to stay over here two years. Let's buy the Duke and take him with us."

*   *   *   *   *

The reaction has come. I knew it would. It always does. It is a mortification to be obliged to admit it in the face of London, and all that we have had done for us, but the fact is we are homesick—wretchedly, bitterly homesick. I remember how, when other people have been here and written that they were homesick, I have sniffed with contempt and have said to myself, "What poor taste! Just wait until *my* turn comes to go to Europe! I'll show them what it is to enjoy every moment of my stay!"

But now—dear me, I can remember that I have made invidious remarks about New York, and have objected to the odors in Chicago, and have hated the Illinois Central turnstiles. But if I could be back in America I would not mind being caught in a turnstile all day. Dear America! Dear Lake Michigan! Dear Chicago!

I have talked the matter over with my sister, and we have decided that it must be the people, for certainly the novelty is not yet worn off of this marvellous London. We like individually nearly every one whom we have met, but as a nation the English are to me an acquired taste—just like olives and German opera.

To explain. My friendly, volatile American feelings are constantly being shocked at the massed and consolidated indifference of English men and women to each other. They care for nobody but themselves. In a certain sense this indifference to other people's opinions is very satisfactory. It makes you feel that no matter how outrageous you wanted to be you could not cause a ripple of excitement or interest— unless Royalty noticed your action. Then London would tread itself to death in its efforts to see and hear you. But if an Englishman entered a packed theatre on his hands with his feet in the air, and thus proceeded to make the rounds of the house, the audience would only give one glance, just to make sure that it was nothing more abnormal than a man in evening dress, carrying his crush-hat between his feet and walking on his hands, and then they would return to their exciting conversation of where they were "going to show after the play." Even the maids who usher would not smile, but would stoop and put his programme between his teeth for him, and turn to the next comer.

The English mind their own business, and we Americans are so used to interfering with each other, and minding everybody's business as well as our own, it makes us very homesick indeed, to find that we can do precisely as we please and be let entirely alone.

The English who have been in America, or those who have a single blessed drop of Irish or Scotch blood in their veins, will quite understand what I mean. Fortunately for us we have found a few of these different sorts, and they have kept us from suicide. They warned us of the differences we would find. One man said to me: "We English do not understand the meaning of the word hospitality compared to you Americans. Now in the States—"

"Stop right there, if you please," I begged, "and say 'America.' It offends me to be called 'the States' quite as much as if you called me 'the Colonies' or 'the Provinces!'"

"You speak as if you were America," he said.

"I am," I replied.

"Now that is just it. You Americans come over here nationally. We English travel individually."

I was so startled at this acute analysis from a man whom I had always regarded as an Englishman that I forgot my manners and I said, "Good heavens, you are not all English, are you?"

"My father was Irish," he said.

"I knew it!" I cried with joy. "Please shake hands with me again. I knew you weren't entirely English after that speech!"

He laughed.

"I will shake hands with you, of course. But I am a typical Britisher. Please believe that."

"I shall not. You are not typical. That was really a clever distinction and quite true."

He looked as if he were going to argue the point with me, so I hurried on. I always get the worst of an argument, so I tried to take his mind off his injury. "Now please go on," I urged. "It sounded so interesting."

"Well, I was only going to say that in America you are, as hosts, quite sincere in wishing us to enjoy ourselves and to like America. Here we will only do our duty by you if you bring letters to us, and we don't care a hang whether you like England or not. We like it, and that's enough."

"I see," I said, with cold chills of aversion for England as a nation creeping over my enthusiasm.

"Now in America," he proceeded, "your host sends his carriage for you, or calls for you, takes you with him, stays by you, introduces you to the people he thinks you would most care to meet, and tells them who and what you are; sees that you have everything that's going, and that you see everything that's going, and then takes you back to your club."

"Then he asks you if you have had a good time, and if you like America!" I supplemented.

"Oh, Lord, yes! He asks you that all the time, and so does everybody else," he said, with a groan.

"Now, you were unkind if you didn't tell him all he wanted you to, for I do assure you it was pure American kindness of heart which made him take all that trouble for you. I know, too, without your telling me, that he introduced you to all the prettiest girls, and gave you a chance to talk to each of them, and only hovered around waiting to take you on to the next one, as soon as he could catch you with ease."

"He did just that. How did you know?"

"Because he was a typical American host, God bless him, and that is the way we do things over there."

"Now here," he went on, "we consider our duty done if we take a man to dine, and then to some reception, where we turn him loose after one or two introductions."

"What a hateful way of doing!" I said, politely.

"It is. It must seem barbarous to you."

"It does."

"Or if you are a woman we send our carriages to let you drive where you like. Or we send you invitations to go to needlework exhibitions where you have to pay five shillings admission."

I said nothing, and he laughed.

"I know they have done that to you," he exclaimed. "Haven't they?"

"I have been delightfully entertained at luncheons and dinners and teas, and I have been introduced to as charming people in London as I ever hope to meet anywhere," I said, stolidly.

"But you won't tell about the needlework. Oh, I say, but that's jolly! Fancy what you said when you began to get those beastly things!" And he laughed again.

"I didn't say anything," I said. Then he roared. Yet he claimed to be a "typical Britisher."

"We mean kindly," he went on. "You mustn't lay it up against us."

"Oh, we don't. We are having a lovely time."

There are times when the truth would be brutal.

Then this oasis of a man, this "typical Britisher," went away, and my sister and I dressed for the theatre. A friend had sent us her box, and assured us that it was perfectly proper for us to go alone. So we went. Up to this time we had not hinted to each other that we were homesick. The play was most amusing, yet we couldn't help watching the audience. Such a bored-looking set, the women with frizzled hair held down by invisible nets, mingling with their eyebrows, and done hideously in the back. Low-necked gowns, exhibiting the most beautiful shoulders in the world. Gorgeous jewels in their hair and gleaming all over their bodices, but among half a dozen emerald, turquoise, and diamond bracelets there would appear a silver-watch bracelet which cost not over ten dollars, and spoiled the effect of all the others.

English women as a race are the worst-dressed women in the world. I saw thousands of them in Piccadilly and Regent

Street, and at Church Parade in the Park, with high, French-heeled slippers over colored stockings. And as to sizes, I should say nines were the average. There are some smaller, but the most are larger.

The Prince of Wales was in the box opposite to ours, and when we were not looking at him we gazed at the impassive faces of the audience. They never smiled. They never laughed. The subtlest points in the play went unnoticed, yet it is one which has had a record run and bids fair to keep the boards for the rest of the season.

Suddenly my sister, although we had not spoken of the homesickness that was weighing us down, touched my arm and said, "Look quick! There's one!"

"Where? Where?"

"Down there just in front of the pit, talking to that bald-headed idiot with the monocle."

"Do you think she is American?" I said, dubiously. I couldn't see her feet. "She might be French. She talks all over."

"No. She is an American girl. See how thin she is. The French are short and fat."

"Look at her face," I said, enviously. "How animated it is. See how it seems to stand out among all the other faces."

"Yet she is only amusing herself. See how stolid that creature looks that she is wasting all her vitality on."

"She has told him some joke and she is laughing at it. He has put his monocle in his other eye in his effort to see the point. He will get it by the next boat. Wish she'd come and tell that joke to me. I'd laugh at it."

My sister eyed me critically.

"You don't look as if you could laugh," she said.

"I wonder what would happen if I should fall dead and drop over into the lap of that fat elephant in pink silk with the red neck," I said, musingly.

"She wouldn't even wink," said my sister, laughingly. "But if you struck her just right you would bounce clear up here again and I could catch you."

"It is just four o'clock in Chicago," I said.

My sister promptly turned her back on me.

"And Billy has just wakened from his nap, and Katy is giving him his food," I went on. (Billy is my sister's baby.) "And then mamma will come into the nursery presently and take him while Katy gets his carriage out, and she will show him my picture and ask him who it is (because she wrote me she always did it at this time), and then he will say, 'Tattah,' which is the sweetest baby word for 'Auntie' I ever heard from mortal lips, and then he will kiss it of his own accord. Mamma wrote that he had blistered it with his kisses, and it's one of the big ones, but I don't care; I'll order a dozen more if he will blister them all. And then she will say, 'Where did mamma and Tattah go?' and he will wave his precious little square hand and say, 'Big boat,' and she says he tries to say, 'Way off'—and, oh, dear, we are 'way off—"

"Stop talking, you fiend," said my sister, from the depths of her handkerchief. "You know I look like a fright when I cry."

"Boo-hoo," was my only reply. And once started, I couldn't stop. That deadly English atmosphere of indifference—and, oh—and everything!

Have you ever been homesick when you couldn't get home? Have you ever wanted to see your mother so that every bone in your body ached? Have you ever been in the state where to see the baby for five minutes you would give everything on earth you had? That was the way I felt about Billy that grewsome night at this amusing play in an English theatre. I had on my best clothes, but after my handkerchief ceased to avail the tears slopped down on my satin gown, and the blisters will remain as a lasting tribute to the contagion of a company of English people out enjoying themselves.

My sister's stern sense of decorum caused her to contain herself until she got home, but I am free to confess that after I once loosed my hold over myself and found what a relief it was, I realized the truth of what our old negro cook used to say when I was a child in the South, and asked her why she howled and cried in such an alarming manner when she "got religion." She used to say, "Lawd, chile, you don't know how soovin' it is to jest bust out awn 'casions lake dese!"

Happy negroes! Happy children, who can "bust out" when their feelings get the better of them! Civilization robs us of many of our acutest pleasures.

That night on the way home from the theatre I learned something. Nobody had ever told me that it is the custom to give the cabby an extra sixpence when one takes a cab late at night, so, on alighting in front of our flower-trimmed lodgings, I reached up, deposited my shilling in his hand, and was turning away, when my footsteps were arrested by my cabby's voice.

Turning, I saw him tossing the despised shilling in his curved palm and saying:

"A shillin'! Twelve o'clock at night! Two ladies in evenin' dress! *You* ought to 'a' gone in a 'bus! A cab's too expensive for *you*! *I* wish you'd 'a' *walked* and I wish it had *rained*!"

With that parting shot he gathered up the lines and drove off, while I leaned up against the door shaking with a laughter which my sister in no wise shared with me. Poor Bee! Things like that jar her so that she can't get any amusement out of them. To her it was terrifying impudence. To me it was a heart-to-heart talk with a London cabby!

Oh, the sweet viciousness of that "*I* wish it had *rained*!" I wonder if that man beats his wife, or if he just converses with her as he does with a recreant fare! Anyway, I loved him.

But if I have discovered nothing else in the brief time since I left my native land, it is worth while to realize the truth of all the poetry and song written on foreign shores about home.

To one accustomed to travel only in America, and to feel at home with all the different varieties of one's countrymen, such sentiments are no more than *vers de societe*. *But* now I know what *Heimweh* is—the home-pain. I can understand that the Swiss really die of it sometimes. The home-pain! Neuralgia, you know, and most other acute pains, attack only one set of nerves. But *Heimweh* hurts all over. There is not a muscle of the body, nor the most remote fibre of the brain, nor a tissue of the heart that does not ache with it. You can't eat. You can't sleep. You can't read or write or talk. It begins with the protoplasm of your soul—and reaches forward to the end of time, and aches every step of the way along. You want to hide your face in a pillow away from everybody and do nothing but weep, but even that does not cure. It seems to be too private to help materially. The only thing I can recommend is to "bust out."

Homesickness is an inexplicable thing. I have heard brides relate how it attacked them unmercifully and without cause in the midst of their honeymoon. Girl students, whose sole aim in life has been to come abroad to study, and who, in finally coming, have fondly dreamed that the gates of Paradise had swung open before their delighted eyes, have been among its earliest and most acutely afflicted victims. No success, no realized ambitions ward it off. Like death, it comes to high and low alike. One woman, whose name became famous with her first concert, told me that she spent the first year over here in tears. Nothing that friends can do, no amount of kindness or hospitality avails as a preventive. You can take bromides and cure insomnia. You can take chloroform, and enough of it will prevent seasickness, but nothing avails for *Heimweh*. And like pride, "let him that thinketh he standeth take heed lest he fall." I have been in the midst of an animated, recital of how homesick I had been the day before, ridiculing myself and my malady with unctuous freedom, when suddenly Billy's little face would seem to rise out of the flowers on the dinner-table, or the patter of his little flying feet as they used to sound in my ear as he fluttered down the long hall to my study, or the darling way he used to ran towards me when I held out my arms and said, "Come, Billy, let Tattah show you the doves," with such an expectant face, and that little scarlet mouth opened to kiss me—oh, it is nothing to anybody else, but it is home to me, and I was only recalled to London and my dinner party when a fresh attack was made on America, and I was called once more to battle for my country.

I have "fought, bled, and died" for home and country more times than I can count since I have been here. I ought to

Lilian Bell

come home with honorable scars and the rank of field-marshal, at least. I never knew how many objectionable features America presented to Englishmen until I became their guest and broke bread at their tables. I cannot eat very much at their dinner parties—I am too busy thinking how to parry their attacks on my America, and especially my Chicago, and my West generally. The English adore Americans, but they loathe America, and I, for one, will not accept a divided allegiance. "Love me, love my dog," is my motto. I go home from their dinners as hungry as a wolf, but covered with Victoria crosses. I am puzzled to know if they really hate Chicago more than any other spot on earth, or if they simply love to hear me fight for it, or if their manners need improving.

I myself may complain of the horrors of our filthy streets, or of the way we tear up whole blocks at once (here in London they only mend a teaspoonful of pavement at a time), or of our beastly winds which tear your soul from your body, but I hope never to sink so low as to permit a lot of foreigners to do it. For even as a Parisian loves his Paris, and as a New Yorker loves his London, so do I love my Chicago.

III

PARIS

It was a fortunate thing, after all, that I went to London first, and had my first great astonishment there. It broke Paris to me gently.

For a month I have been in this city of limited republicanism; this extraordinary example of outward beauty and inward uncleanness; this bewildering cosmopolis of cheap luxuries and expensive necessities; this curious city of contradictions, where you might eat your breakfast from the streets—they are so clean—but where you must close your eyes to the spectacles of the curbstones; this beautiful, whited sepulchre, where exists the unwritten law, "Commit any offence you will, provided you submerge it in poetry and flowers"; this exponent of outward observances, where a gentleman will deliberately push you into the street if he wishes to pass you in a crowd, but where his action is condoned by his inexpressible manner of raising his hat to you, and the heartfelt sincerity of his apology; where one man will run a mile to restore a lost franc, but if you ask him to change a gold piece he will steal five; where your eyes are ravished with the beauty, and the greenness, and the smoothness and apparent ease of living of all its inhabitants; where your mind is filled with the pictures, the music, the art, the general atmosphere of culture and wit; where the cooking is so good but so elusive, and where the shops are so bewitching that you have spent your last dollar without thinking, and you are obliged to cable for a new letter of credit from home before you know it—this is Paris.

Paris is very educational. I can imagine its influence broadening some people so much that their own country could never be ample enough to cover them again. I can imagine it narrowing others so that they would return to America more of Puritans than ever. It is amusing, it is fascinating, it is exciting, it is corrupting. The French must be the most curious people on earth. How could even heavenly ingenuity create a more uncommon or bewildering contradiction and combination? Make up your mind that they are as simple as children when you see their innocent picnicking along the boulevards and in the parks with their whole families, yet you dare not trust yourself to hear what they are saying. Believe that they are cynical, and *fin de siecle*, and skeptical of all women when you hear two men talk, and the next day you hear that one of them has shot himself on the grave of his sweetheart. Believe that politeness is the ruling characteristic of the country because a man kisses your hand when he takes leave of you. But marry him, and no insult as regards other women is too low for him to heap upon you. Believe that the French men are sympathetic because they laugh and cry openly at the theatre. But appeal to their chivalry, and they will rescue you from one discomfort only to offer you a worse. The French have sentimentality, but not sentiment. They have gallantry, but not chivalry. They have vanity, but not pride. They have religion, but not morality. They are a combination of the wildest extravagance and the strictest parsimony. They cultivate the ground so close to the railroad tracks that the trains almost run over their roses, and yet they leave a Place de la Concorde in the heart of the city.

You can buy the wing of a chicken at a butcher's and take it home to cook it. But your bill at a restaurant will appall you. Water is the most precious and exclusive drink you can order in Paris. Imagine that—you who let the water run to cool it! In Paris they actually pay for water in their houses by the quart.

Artichokes, and truffles, and mushrooms, and silk stockings, and kid gloves are so cheap here that it makes you blink your eyes. But eggs, and cream, and milk are luxuries. Silks and velvets are bewilderingly inexpensive. But cotton stuffs are from America, and are extravagances. They make them up into "costumes," and trim them with velvet ribbon. Never by any chance could you be supposed to send cotton frocks to be washed every week. The luxury of fresh, starched muslin dresses and plenty of shirt-waists is unknown.

I never shall overcome the ecstasies of laughter which assail me when I see varieties of coal exhibited in tiny shop windows, set forth in high glass dishes, as we exploit chocolates at home. But well they may respect it, for it is really very much cheaper to freeze to death than to buy coal in Paris.

The reason of all this is the city tax on every chicken, every carrot, every egg brought into Paris. Every mouthful of food is taxed. This produces an enormous revenue, and this is why the streets are so clean; it is why the asphalt is as smooth as a ballroom floor; it is why the whole of Paris is as beautiful as a dream.

In fact, the city has ideas of cleanliness which its middle-class inhabitants do not share. On a rainy day in Paris the absurdly hoisted dresses will expose to your view all varieties of trimmed, ruffled, and lace petticoats, which would undeniably be benefited by a bath. All the *lingerie* has

Lilian Bell

ribbons in it, and sometimes I think they are never intended to be taken out.

When I was at the chateau of a friend not long ago she overheard her maid apologizing to two sisters of charity, for the presence of a bath-tub in her mistress's dressing-room: "You must not blame madame la marquise for bathing every day. She is not more untidy than I, and I, God knows, wash myself but twice a year. It is just a habit of hers which she caught from the English."

My friend called to her sharply, and told her she need not apologize for her bathing, to which the maid replied, in a tone of meek justification, "But if madame la marquise only knew how she was regarded by the people for this habit of hers!"

I like the way the French take their amusements. At the theatre they laugh and applaud the wit of the hero and hiss the villain. They shout their approval of a duel and weep aloud over the death of the aged mother. When they drive in the Bois they smile and have an air of enjoyment quite at variance with the bored expression of English and Americans who have enough money to own carriages. We drove in Hyde Park in London the day before we came to Paris, and nearly wept with sympathy for the unspoken grief in the faces of the unfortunate rich who were at such pains to enjoy themselves.

The second day from that we had a delightful drive in the Bois in Paris.

"How glad everybody seems to be we have come!" I said to my sister. "See how pleased they all look."

I was enchanted at their gay faces. I felt like bowing right and left to them, the way queens and circus girls do.

I never saw such handsome men as I saw in London. I never saw such beautiful women as I see in Paris.

The Bois has never been so smart as it was the past season, for the horrible fire of the Bazar de la Charite put an end to the Paris season, and left those who were not personally bereaved no solace but the Bois. Consequently, the costumes one saw between five and seven on that one beautiful boulevard were enough to set one wild. I always wished that my neck turned on a pivot and that I had eyes set like a coronet all around my head. My sister and I were in a constant state of ecstasy and of clutching each other's gowns, trying to see every one who passed. But it was of no use. Although they drove slowly on purpose to be seen, if you tried to focus your glance on each one it seemed as if they drove like lightning, and you got only astigmatism for your pains. I always came home from the Bois with a headache and a stiff neck.

I never dreamed of such clothes even in my dreams of heaven. But the French are an extravagant race. There was hardly a gown worn last season which was not of the most delicate texture, garnished with chiffon and illusion and tulle—the most crushable, airy, inflammable, unserviceable material one can think of. Now, I am a utilitarian. When I see a white gown I always wonder if it will wash. If I see lace on the foot ruffle of a dress I think how it will sound when the wearer steps on it going up-stairs. But anything would be serviceable to wear driving in a victoria in the Bois between five and seven, and as that is where I have seen the most beautiful costumes I have no right to complain, or to thrust at them my American ideas of usefulness. This rage of theirs for beauty is what makes a perpetual honeymoon for the eyes of every inch of France. The way they study color and put

Lilian Bell

greens together in their landscape gardening makes one think with horror of our prairies and sagebrush.

The eye is ravished with beauty all over Paris. The clean streets, the walks between rows of trees for pedestrians, the lanes for bicyclists, the paths through tiny forests, right in Paris, for equestrians, and on each side the loveliest trees—trees everywhere except where there are fountains—but what is the use of trying to describe a beauty which has staggered braver pens than mine, and which, after all, you must see to appreciate?

The Catholic observances one sees everywhere in Paris are most interesting. When a funeral procession passes, every man takes off his hat and stands watching it with the greatest respect.

In May the streets are full of sweet-faced little girls on their way to their first communion. They were all in white, bareheaded, except for their white veils, white shoes, white gloves, and the dearest look of importance on their earnest little faces. It was most touching.

In all months, however, one sees the comical sight of a French bride and bridegroom, in all the glory of their bridal array—white satin, veil, and orange blossoms—driving through the streets in open cabs, and hugging and kissing each other with an unctuous freedom which is apt to throw a conservative American into a spasm of laughter. Indeed, the frank and candid way that love-making goes on in public among the lower classes is so amazing that at first you think you never in this world will become accustomed to it, but you get accustomed to a great many strange sights in Paris. If a kiss explodes with unusual violence in a cab near mine it sometimes scares the horse, but it no longer disturbs me in the least. My nervousness over that sort of thing has entirely worn off.

I have had but one adventure, and that was of a simple and primitive character, which seemed to excite no one but myself. They say that there is no drunkenness in France. If that is so then this cabman of mine had a fit of some kind. Perhaps, though, he was only a beast. Most of the cabmen here are beasts. They beat their poor horses so unmercifully that I spend quite a good portion of my time standing up in the cab and arguing with them. But the only efficacious argument I have discovered is to tell them that they will get no *pourboire* if they beat the horse. That seems to infuse more humanity into them than any number of Scripture texts.

On this occasion my cabman, for no reason whatever, suddenly began to beat his horse in the hatefulest way, leaning down with his whip and striking the horse underneath, as we were going downhill on the Rue de Freycinet. I screamed at him, but he pretended not to hear. The cab rocked from side to side, the horse was galloping, and this brute beating him like a madman. It made me wild. I was being bounced around like corn in a popper and in imminent danger of being thrown to the pavement.

People saw my danger, but nobody did anything—just looked, that was all. I saw that I must save myself if there was any saving going to be done. So with one last trial of my lungs I shrieked at the cabman, but the cobblestones were his excuse, and he kept on. So I just stood up and knocked his hat off with my parasol!—his big, white, glazed hat. It was glorious! He turned around in a fury and pulled up his horse, with a torrent of French abuse and impudence which scared me nearly to death. I thought he might strike me.

So I pulled my twitching lips into a distortion which passed muster with a Paris cabman for a smile, and begged his pardon so profusely that he relented and didn't kill me.

I often blush for the cheap Americans with loud voices and provincial speech, and general commonness, whom one meets over here; but with all their faults they cannot approach the vulgarities at table which I have seen in Paris. In all America we have no such vulgar institution as their *rince-bouche*—an affair resembling a two-part finger-bowl, with the water in a cup in the middle. At fashionable tables, men and women in gorgeous clothes, who speak four or five languages, actually rinse their mouths and gargle at the table, and then slop the water thus used back into these bowls. The first time I saw this I do assure you I would not have been more astonished if the next course had been stomach pumps.

And as for the toothpick habit! Let no one ever tell me that that atrocity is American! Here it goes with every course, and without the pretended decency of holding one's *serviette* before one's mouth, which, in my opinion, is a mere affectation, and aggravates the offence.

But the most shameless thing in all Europe is the marriage question. To talk with intelligent, clever, thinking men and women, who know the secret history of all the famous international marriages, as well as the high contracting parties, who will relate the price paid for the husband, and who the intermediary was, and how much commission he or she received, is to make you turn faint and sick at the mere thought, especially if you happen to come from a country where they once fought to abolish the buying and selling of human beings. But our black slaves were above buying and selling themselves or their children. It remains for civilized Europe of our time to do this, and the highest and proudest of her people at that.

It is not so shocking to read about it in glittering generalities.

I knew of it in a vague way, just as I knew the history of the massacre of Saint Bartholomew. I thought it was too bad that so many people were killed, and I also thought it a pity that Frenchmen never married without a *dot*. But when it comes to meeting the people who had thus bargained, and the moment their gorgeous lace and satin backs were turned to hear some one say, "You are always so interested in that sort of thing, have you heard what a scandal was caused by the marriage of those two?"—then it ceases to be history; then it becomes almost a family affair.

"How could a marriage between two unattached young people cause a scandal?" I asked, with my stupid, primitive American ideas.

"Oh, the bride's mother refused to pay the commission to the intermediary," was the airy reply. "It came near getting into the papers."

At the Jubilee garden party at Lady Monson's I saw the most beautiful French girl I have seen in Paris. She was superb. In America she would have been a radiant, a triumphant beauty, and probably would have acquired the insolent manners of some of our spoiled beauties. Instead of that, however, she was modest, even timid-looking, except for her queenly carriage. Her gown was a dream, and a dream of a dress at a Paris garden party means something.

"What a tearing beauty!" I said to my companion. "Who is she?"

"Yes, poor girl!" he said. "She is the daughter of the Comtesse N—. One of the prettiest girls in Paris. Not a sou, however; consequently she will never marry. She will probably go into a convent."

"But why? Why won't she marry? Why aren't all the men crazy about her? Why don't you marry her?"

"Marry a girl without a *dot*? Thank you, mademoiselle. I am an expense to myself. My wife must not be an additional encumbrance."

"But surely," I said, "somebody will want to marry her, if no nobleman will."

"Ah, yes, but she is of noble blood, and she must not marry beneath her. No one in her own class will marry her, so"—a shrug—"the convent! See, her chances are quite gone. She has been out five years now."

I could have cried. Every word of it was quite true. I thought of the dozens of susceptible and rich American men I knew who would have gone through fire and water for her, and who, although they have no title to give her, would have made her adoring and adorable husbands, and I seriously thought of offering a few of them to her for consideration! But alas, there are so many ifs and ands, and—well, I didn't.

I only sighed and said, "Well, I suppose such things are common in France, but I do assure you such things are impossible in America."

"Such things as what, mademoiselle?"

"This cold-blooded bartering," I said. "American men are above it."

"Are American girls above selling themselves, mademoiselle? Do you see that poor, pitifully plain little creature there, in that dress which cost a fortune? Do you see how ill she carries it? Do you see her unformed, uncertain manner?

Her husband is the one I just had the honor of presenting to you, who is now talking to the beauty you so much admire."

"He shows good taste in spite of his marriage," I said.

"Certainly. But his wife is your countrywoman. That is the last famous international marriage, and the most vulgar of the whole lot. Listen, mademoiselle, and I will tell you the exact truth of the whole affair.

"She came over here with letters to Paris friends, and when it became known that one of the richest heiresses in America was here, naturally all the mammas with marriageable sons were anxious to see her. She was invited everywhere, but as she could not speak French, and as she was as you see her, her success could not be said to be great. No, but that made no difference. The Duchesse de Z—was determined that her son should marry the rich heiress. As she expected to remain here a year or more, and the young Duc de Z—made a wry face, she did not press the matter. Then the heiress went into a convent to learn French, and the Duchesse went to see her very often and took her to drive, and did her son's part as well as she could.

"Suddenly, to the amazement of everybody, the heiress sailed for America without a word of warning. The Duchesse was furious. 'You must follow her,' she said to her son. 'We cannot let so much money escape.' The son said he would be hanged if he went to America, or if he would marry such a monkey, and as for her money, she could go anywhere she pleased with it, or words to that effect. So that ended the affair of the Duc de Z—. When the other impecunious young nobles heard that the Duchesse no longer had any claims upon the American's money they got together and said, 'Somebody must marry her and divide with the rest. We can't all marry her, but we can all have a share from whoever does. Now we will draw lots to see who must go to America and marry her.' The lot fell to the Baron de X—, but he had no money for the journey. So all the others raised what money they could and loaned it to him, and took his notes for it, with enormous interest, payable after his marriage. He sailed away, and within eight months he had married her, but he has not paid those notes because his wife won't give him the money! And these gentlemen are furious! Good joke, I call it."

"What a shameful thing!" I said. "I wonder if that girl knew how she was being married!"

"Of course she knew! At least, she might have known. She was rich and she was plain. How could she hope to gain one of the proudest titles in France without buying it?"

"I wonder if she could have known!" I said, again.

"It would not have prevented the marriage, would it, mademoiselle, if she had?"

"Indeed it would!" I said (but I don't know whether it would or not). He shrugged his shoulders.

"America is very different from Europe, then, mademoiselle. Here it would have made no difference. When a great amount of money is to be placed, one must not have too many scruples."

"If she did know," I said, with a fervor which was lost upon him, "believe this, whether you can understand it or not: she was not a typical American girl."

I had, as usual, many more words which he deserved to have had said to him, but education along this line takes too much time. I ought to have begun this great work with his great-grandparents.

*   *   *   *   *

What any one can see about Dinard to like is a mystery to me! Is it possible that one who has spent a month there could ever be lured back again? There is a beautiful journey from Paris across France southwesterly to the coast, through odd little French villages, vineyards, poppy-fields, and rose-gardens, across shining rivulets and through an undulating landscape, all so lovely that it is no wonder that one expects all this beauty to lead up to a climax. But what a disappointment Dinard is to one's enthusiastic anticipations! This famous watering-place has to my mind not one solitary redeeming feature. It has no excuse for being famous. It has not even one happy accident about it as a peg to hang its fame upon, like some writers' first novels. Dinard simply goes on being famous, nobody knows why. And to go there, after reading pages about it in the papers and hearing people speak of Dinard as Mohammedans whisper sacredly of Mecca, is like meeting celebrities. You wonder what under the sun—what in the world—how in the name of Heaven such ugly, stupid, uninteresting, heavy, dull, and insufferably ordinary persons are allowed to become famous by an overruling and beneficent Providence! I have met many celebrities, and I have been to Dinard. I have had my share of disappointments.

To begin with, Dinard is not sufficiently picturesque. There are but one or two pretty vistas and three or four points of view. Then it is not typically French. It is inhabited partly by English families who cross the Channel yearly from Southampton and Portsmouth, and who take with them their nine uninteresting daughters, with long front teeth and ill-hanging duck skirts, and partly by Americans who go to

Dinard as they go to the Eiffel Tower; not that either is particularly interesting, but they had heard of these places before they came over. The only really interesting thing within five miles of Dinard is that, off St. Malo, on the island of Grand Be, Chateaubriand is buried. But as this really belongs more to the attractions of St. Malo than to Dinard, and nobody who spends summers at Dinard ever mentioned Chateaubriand in my presence, or honored his tomb by a visit, it is pure charity on my part to ascribe this solitary point of real interest to Dinard. For, after all, Chateaubriand does not belong to it. Which logic reminds me forcibly of the plea entered by the defence in a suit for borrowing a kettle: "In the first place, I never borrowed his kettle; in the second place, it was whole when I returned it; and, in the third place, it was cracked when I got it."

So with Chateaubriand and Dinard. Then Dinard has none of the dash and go of other watering-places. There is nothing to do except to bathe mornings and watch the people win or lose two francs at *petits chevaux* in the evenings. Not wildly exciting, that. Consequently, you soon begin to stagnate with the rest.

You grow more and more stupid as the weeks pass, and at the end of a month you cease to think. From that time on you do not have such a bad time—that is to say, you do not suffer so acutely, because you have now got down to the level of the people who go back to Dinard the next year.

We came away. The hotels are among the worst on earth— musty, old-fashioned, and villainously expensive—and one of the happiest moments in my life was the day when I left Dinard for Mont St. Michel. Mont St. Michel is one of the most out-of-the-way, un-get-at-able places I found in all Europe; but, oh, how it rewards one who arrives!

Mont St. Michel is too well known to need a description. But to go from Dinard requires, first of all, that one must go by boat over to St. Malo, thence by train; change cars, and alight finally at a lonely little station, behind which stands a sort of vehicle—a cross between a London omnibus and a hay-wagon. You scramble to the top of this as best you may. Nobody helps you. The Frenchman behind you crowds forward and climbs up ahead of you and holds you back with his umbrella while he hauls his fat wife up beside him. Then you clamber up by the hub of the wheel and by sundry awkward means which remind you of climbing a stone wall when you were a child. You take any seat left, which the Frenchmen do not want, the horses are put to, and away you go over a smooth sandy road for eleven miles, with the sea crawling up on each side of you over the dunes.

Suddenly, without warning, you come squarely upon Mont St. Michel, rising solidly five hundred feet from nowhere. There is a whole town in this fortress, built upon this rock, street above street, like a flight of stairs, and house piled up behind house, until on the very top there is one of the most famous cathedrals in the world; and as you thread its maze of vaulted chambers and dungeons and come to its gigantic tower you are lost in absolute wonder at the building of it.

Where did they get the material? And when got, what human ingenuity could raise those enormous blocks of stone to that vast height? How those cannon swept all approach by land or sea as far as the eye could reach! It would require superb courage in an enemy to come within reach of that grim sentinel of France, manned by her warrior monks. What secrets those awful dungeons might relate! Here political crimes were avenged with all the cruelty of Siberian exile. Here prisoners wore their lives away in black solitude, no ray of light penetrating their darkness.

The story is told that one poor wretch was eaten alive by gigantic rats, and they have a ghastly reproduction of it in wax, which makes you creepy for a week after you have seen it. Nowhere in all Europe did I see a place which impressed its wonder and its history of horror upon me as did the cathedral dungeon of Mont St. Michel. Its situation was so impregnable, its capacity so vast, its silence and isolation from the outer world so absolute.

All Russia does not boast a situation so replete with possible and probable misery and anguish such as were suggested to my mind here.

But the wonder and charm of the compact little town which clings like a limpet to its base are more than can be expressed on the written page. It is like climbing the uneven stairs of some vast and roofless ancient palace, upon each floor of which dwell families who have come in and roofed over the suites of rooms and made houses out of them. The stairs lead you, not from floor to floor, but from bakery to carpenter-shop, from the blacksmith's to the telegraph-office.

The streets are paved with large cobblestones, to prevent cart-wheels from slipping, and are so narrow that I often had to stand up at afternoon tea with my cup in one hand and my chair in the other, to let a straining, toiling little donkey pass me, gallantly hauling his load of fagots up an incline of forty-five degrees.

The famous inn here is kept by Madame Poularde, who can cook so marvellously that she is one of the wonders of Normandy. Her kitchen faces the main street; you simply step over the threshold as you hear the beating of eggs, and there, over an immense open fire, which roars gloriously up the chimney, are the fowls twirling on their strings and dripping deliciously into the pans which sizzle complainingly on the coals beneath.

Presently the roaring ceases, the fresh coals are flattened down, and into a skillet, with a handle five feet long, is dropped the butter, which melts almost instantly. A fat little red-faced boy pushes the skillet back and forth to keep the butter from burning. The frantic beating of eggs comes nearer and nearer. The shrill voice of Madame Poularde screams voluble French at her assistants. She boxes somebody's ears, snatches the eggs, gives them one final puffy beating, which causes them to foam up and overflow, and at that exciting moment out they bubble into the smoking skillet, the handle of which she seizes at the identical moment that she lets go of the empty bowl with one hand and pushes the red-faced boy over backward with the other. It is legerdemain! But then, *how* she manages that skillet! How her red cheeks flush, her black eyes sparkle, and her plump hands guide that ship of state!

We are all so excited that we get horribly in her way and almost fall into the fire in our anxiety. She stirs and coaxes and coquettes with the lovely foamy mass until it becomes as light as the yellow down on a fledgling's wings. She calls it an omelette, but she is scrambling those eggs! Then when it is almost done she screams at us to take our places. The red-faced boy rings a huge bell, and we all tumble madly up the narrow stairs to the dining-room, where a score of assorted tourists are seated. *They* get that first omelette because they behaved better than we did, and were more orderly. There are half a dozen little maids who attend us. They give us bread and bring our wine and get our plates all ready, for, behold, we can hear below the beating of the eggs and the sizzling of the butter, and presently Madame Poularde's scream and slap, and we know that our omelette is on the way!

There were scores of bridal parties there when we were, for Mont St. Michel seems to be the Niagara of France, and really one could hardly imagine a more charming place for a honeymoon. Indeed, for a newly married couple, for boy and girl, for spinsters and bachelors, ay, even for Darby and Joan, Mont St. Michel has attractions. All sorts and conditions of men here find the most romantic and interesting spot to be found in the whole of France.

While here we got telegrams telling us of the assembling of our friends at a house-party at a chateau in the south of France which once had belonged to Charles VII. So without waiting for anything more we wired a joyful acceptance and set out. We did, however, stop over a few hours at Blois, in order to see the chateau there. We really did Blois in a spirit of Baedeker, for we were crazy to see Velor, in order not to miss an inch of the good times which we knew would riot there. But virtue was its own reward, for as we were looking into the depths of the first real oubliette which I ever had seen, and I was just shivering with the vision of that fiendish Catharine de' Medici who used to drop people into these holes every morning before breakfast, just as an appetizer, we heard a most blood-curdling shriek, and there stood that wretched Jimmie watching us from an open door, waving his Baedeker at us, with Mrs. Jimmie's lovely Madonna smile seen over his shoulder.

No one who has not felt the awful pangs of homesickness abroad has any idea of the joy with which one greets intimate friends in Europe. I believe that travel in Europe has done more toward the riveting of lukewarm American friendships than any other thing in the world.

The Jimmies have often appeared upon my pathway like angels of light, and at Blois we simply loved them, for Blois is not only gloomy, but it has a most ghastly history. The murder of the Duc de Guise and his brother, by order of King Henry III., took place here. They show one the rooms where the murder was committed, the door through which the murderer entered, and the private *cabinet de travail* where the king waited for the news.

Here, also, Margaret of Valois married Henry of Navarre, and Charles, Duc d'Alencon, married Margaret of Anjou. But one hardly ever thinks of the weddings which occurred here for the horrors which overshadow them. How fitting that Marie de' Medici should have been imprisoned here, and my ancient enemy, Catharine, that queen-mother who perched her children on thrones as carelessly and as easily as did Napoleon and Queen Louise of Denmark—that Catharine should have died here, "unregretted and unlamented," was too lovely!

Then we left the magnificent old castle and took the train for Port-Boulet, where the Marquise met us with her little private omnibus, holding eight, drawn by handsome American horses. They were new horses and young, and the Marquise said that Charles found them quite unmanageable. Jimmie watched him drive them around a moment or two before they could be made to stand, then he broke out laughing. The Marquise was so disgusted at the way they see-sawed that she said she was going to sell them.

"Sell them!" cried Jimmie. "Why, all in the world that's the matter with those poor brutes is that they don't speak French! Let *me* drive them!"

So the Marquise saved Charles's vanity by saying that monsieur wished to try the new horses. Jimmie climbed upon the box, and gathered up the reins, saying, "So, old boy, you don't like the dratted language any better than I do. Steady now, boy! *Giddap*!" Whereat the pretty creatures pricked up their ears, pranced a little, then sprang into their collars, and we were off along the lovely river road at a spanking pace and with as smooth and even a gait as the most experienced roadsters.

We could hear Charles's polite compliments to Jimmie on his driving, and Jimmie's awful French, as he assured Charles that the horses were all right, "*tres gentils*" and "*tres jolis*." "*Ne dites jamais 'doucement' aux chevaux americains. Dites 'whoa,' et ils arreteront, et quand vous dites 'Giddap,' ils marcheront bien. Savez?*" At which Charles obediently practised "Whoa!" and "Giddap!" while we felt ourselves pulled up and started off, as the object-lesson demanded, but amid shrieks of laughter which quite upset Charles's dignity.

Finally, we whirled in across the moat and under the great gate to the chateau, and found ourselves in the billiard-room of Velor, with a big open fire, in front of which lay a pile of dogs and around which we all gathered shiveringly, for the day was chilly.

That charming billiard-room at Velor! It is not so grand as the rest of the chateau, but everybody loves it best of all. It is on the ground floor, and it has a writing-desk and two or three little work-tables and several sofas and heaps of easy-chairs, and here everybody came to read or write or sew or play billiards. And as to afternoon tea! Not one of us could have been hired to drink it in the salons up-stairs. In fact, so many of us insisted upon being in the billiard-room that there never was room for a free play of one's cue, for somebody was always in the way, and it was rather discouraging to hear a woman doing embroidery say, "Don't hit this ball. Take some other stroke, can't you? Your cue will strike me in the eye."

Dunham, the eighteen-year-old son of the Marquise, was

teaching me billiards, but his manners were so beautiful that he always pretended that to stick to one's own ball was a mere arbitrary rule of the game, so he permitted me to play with either ball, which made it easiest for me, or which caused least discomfort to those sitting uncomfortably near the table. A dear boy, that Dunham! He had but one fault, and that was that he *would* wear cerise and scarlet cravats, and his hair was red—so uncompromisingly red, of such an obstinate and determined red, that his mother often said, "Come here, Dunham, dear, and light up this corner of the room with your sunny locks. It is too dark to see how to thread my needle!" Such was his amiability that I am sure he enjoyed it, for he always went promptly, and called her "*Mon amour*," and slyly kissed her when he thought we were not looking.

All our remarks upon his red ties fell upon unheeding ears, until one day I bribed his man to bring me every one of them. These I distributed among the women guests, and when, the next morning, Dunham came in complaining that he couldn't find any of his red ties, lo! every woman in the room was wearing one; and to our credit be it spoken that he failed to get any of them back, and never, to my knowledge at least, wore a scarlet tie again.

Velor is historic. After it passed out of the hands of Charles VII.—I have slept in his room, but I must say that he was unpleasantly short if that bed fitted him!—it was bought by the old miser Nivelau, whose daughter, Eugenie Belmaison, was the girl Balzac wished to marry. In a rage at being rejected by her father he wrote *Eugenie Grandet*, and several of the articles, such as her work-box, of which Balzac makes mention, are in the possession of the Marquise.

Every available room in the Velor was filled with our party. Each day we drove in the brake to visit some ancient chateau, such as Azay-le-Rideau, Islette, Chinon, or the Abbey of Fontevreault, finding the roads and scenery in Touraine the most delightful one can imagine.

Fontevreault was originally an abbey, and a most powerful one, being presided over by daughters of kings or women of none but the highest rank, and these noble women held the power of life and death over all the country which was fief to Fontevreault.

Velor was once fief to Fontevreault, but the abbey is now turned into a prison.

They took away our cameras before they allowed us to enter, but we saw some of the prisoners, of whom there were one thousand. The real object of our visit, however, was to see the tombs of Henry II. and of my beloved Richard the Lion-hearted, who are both buried at Fontevreault. To go to Fontevreault, we were obliged to cross the river Vienne on the most curious little old ferry, which was only a raft with the edges turned up. Charles drove the brake on to this raft, but we preferred, after one look into the eyes of the American horses, to climb down and trust to our own two feet.

We gave and attended breakfasts with the owners of neighboring chateaux, drove into Saumur to the theatre or to dine with the officers of the regiment stationed there, and had altogether a perfect visit. I have made many visits and have been the guest of many hostesses, most of them charming ones, hence it is no discourtesy to them and but a higher compliment to the Marquise when I assert that she is one of the most perfect hostesses I ever met.

A thorough woman of the world, having been presented at three courts and speaking five languages, yet her heart is as untouched by the taint of worldliness, her nature as unembittered by her sorrows, as if she were a child just opening her eyes to society. One of the cleverest of women, she is both humorous and witty, with a gift of mimicry which would have made her a fortune on the stage.

Her servants idolize her, manage the chateau to suit themselves, which fortunately means to perfection, and look upon her as a beloved child who must be protected from all the minor trials of life. She has rescued the most of them from some sort of discomfort, and their gratitude is boundless. Like the majority of the nobility, the peasants of France are royalists. The middle class, the *bourgeoisie*, are the backbone of the republic.

The servants are stanch Catholics and long for a monarchy again. The Marquise apologized to them for our being heretics, and told them that while we were not Christians (Catholics), yet we tried to be good, and in the main turned out a fair article, but she entreated their clemency and their prayers for her guests. So we had the satisfaction of being ardently prayed for all the time we were there, and of being complimented occasionally by her maid, Marie, an old Normandie peasant seventy years old, for an act on our part now and then which savored of real Christianity. And once when we had private theatricals, and I dressed as a nun, Marie never found out for half the evening that I was not one of the Sisters who frequently came to the chateau, but kept crossing herself whenever she saw me; and when she discovered me she told me, with tears in her eyes, it really was a thousand pities that I would not renounce the world and become a Christian, because I looked so much like a "religieuse."

We went in oftenest to Chinon—always on market day; some of us on horseback, some on wheels, while the rest drove. Chinon is the fortress chateau where Jeanne d'Arc came to see Charles VII. to try to interest him in her plans. Its ruins stand high up on a bluff overlooking the town, and beneath it in an open square is the very finest and most spirited equestrian statue I ever saw. It is of Jeanne d'Arc, and I only regret that the photograph I took of it is too small to show its fire and spirit and the mad rush of the horse, and the glorious, generous pose of the noble martyr's outstretched arms, as she seems to be in the act of sacrificing her life to her country. There is the divinest patriotism in every line of it.

We saw it on a beautiful crisp day in November. It was our Thanksgiving day at home. We drove along the lovely river-road from Chinon to Velor, and upon our arrival we discovered that the Marquise had arranged an American Thanksgiving dinner for us, sending even to America for certain delicacies appropriate to the season. It was a most gorgeous Thanksgiving dinner, for, aside from the turkey, lo! there appeared a peacock in all its magnificent plumage, sitting there looking so dressy with all his feathers on that we quite blushed for the state of the turkey.

A month of Paris, and then I long for fresh fields and pastures new. Of course there is nowhere like Paris for clothes or to eat. But when one has got all the clothes one can afford and is no longer hungry, having acquired a chronic indigestion from too intimate a knowledge of Marguery's and Ledoyen's, what is there to do but to leave?

Paris is essentially a holiday town, but I get horribly tired of too long a holiday, and after the newness is worn off one discovers that it is the superficiality of it all that palls. The people are superficial; their amusements are feathery—even the beauty of it all is "only skin deep."

Therefore, after one glimpse of Poland, the pagan in my nature called me to the East, and six months of Paris have only intensified my longing to get away—to get to something solid; to find myself once more with the serious thinkers of the world.

In the mean time Bee has deserted me for the more interesting society of Billy, and now she writes me long letters so filled with his sayings and doings that I must move on or I shall die of homesickness. I have decided on Russia and the Nile, taking intermediate countries by the way. This is entirely Billy's fault.

When I first decided to go to Russia, I supposed, of course, that I could induce the Jimmies to go with me, but, to my consternation, they revolted, and gently but firmly expressed their determination to go to Egypt by way of Italy. So I have taken a companion, and if all goes well we shall meet the Jimmies on the terrace of Shepheard's in February.

I packed three trunks in my very best style, only to have Mrs. Jimmie regard my work with a face so full of disapproval that it reminded me of Bee's. She then proceeded to put "everything any mortal could possibly want" into one trunk, with what seemed to me supernatural skill and common-sense, calmly sending the other two to be stored at Munroe's. I don't like to disparage Mrs. Jimmie's idea of what I need, but it does seem to me that nearly everything I have wanted here in Berlin is "stored at Munroe's."

My companion and I, with faultless arithmetic, calculated our expenses and drew out what we considered "plenty of French money to get us to the German frontier." Then Jimmie took my companion and Mrs. Jimmie took me to the train.

Their cab got to the station first, and when we came up Jimmie was grinning, and my companion looked rather sheepish.

"I didn't have enough money to pay the extra luggage," she whispered. "I had to borrow of Mr. Jimmie."

"That's just like you," I said, severely. "Now *I* drew more than you did."

Just then Jimmie came up with *my* little account.

"Forty-nine francs extra luggage," he announced.

"What?" I gasped, "on that *one* trunk?" How grateful I was at that moment for the two stored at Munroe's!

"Oh, Jimmie," I cried, "I haven't got *near* enough! You'll *have* to lend me twenty francs!"

My companion smiled in sweet revenge, and has been almost impossible to travel with since then, but we are one in our rage against paying extra luggage. Just think of buying your clothes once and then paying for them over and over again in every foreign country you travel through! Our clothes will be priceless heirlooms by the time we get home. We can never throw them away. They will be too valuable.

The Jimmies have been so kind to us that we nearly choked over leaving them, but we consoled ourselves after the train left, and proceeded to draw the most invidious comparisons between French sleeping-cars and the rolling palaces we are accustomed to at home. I am ashamed to think that I have made unpleasant remarks upon the discomforts of travel in America. Oh, how ungrateful I have been for past mercies!

My companion is very patient, as a rule, but I heard her restlessly tossing around in her berth, and I said, "What's the matter?"

"Oh, nothing much. But don't you think they have arranged the knobs in these mattresses in very curious places?'"

Well, it *was* a little like sleeping on a wood-pile during a continuous earthquake. But that was nothing compared to the news broken to us about eleven o'clock that our luggage would be examined at the German frontier at five o'clock in the morning. That meant being wakened at half past four. But it was quite unnecessary, for we were not asleep.

It was cold and raining. I got up and dressed for the day. But my companion put her seal-skin on over her dressing-gown, and perched her hat on top of that hair of hers, and looked ready to cope with Diana herself.

"They'll ruin my things if they unpack them," I said.

"You just keep still and let me manage things," she answered. So I did. I made myself as small as possible and watched her. She selected her victim and smiled on him most charmingly. He was tearing open the trunk of a fat American got up in gray flannel and curl-papers. He dropped her tray and hurried up to my companion.

"Have you anything to declare, madam?" he asked.

"Tell him absolutely nothing," she whispered to me. I obeyed, but he never took his eyes from her. She was tugging at the strap of her trunk in apparently wild eagerness to get it open. She frowned and panted a little to show how hard it was, and he bounded forward to help her. Then she smiled at him, and he blinked his eyes and tucked the strap in and chalked her trunk, with a shrug. He hadn't opened it. She kept her eye on him and pointed to my trunk, and he chalked that. Then seven pieces of hand luggage, and he chalked them all. Then she smiled on him again, and I thanked him, but he didn't seem to hear me, and she nodded her thanks and pulled me down a long stone corridor to the dining-room where we could get some coffee.

At the door I looked back. The customs officer was still looking after my companion, but she never even saw it.

The dining-room was full of smoke, but the coffee and my first taste of zwieback were delicious. Then we went out through a narrow doorway to the train, where we were jostled by Frenchmen with their habitual "*Pardon!*" (which partially reconciles you to being walked on), and knocked into by monstrous Germans, who sent us spinning without so much as a look of apology, and both of whom puffed their tobacco smoke directly in our faces. It was still dark and the rain was whimpering down on the car-roof, and, take it all in all, the situation was far from pleasant, but we are hard to depress, and our spirits remain undaunted.

It was so stuffy in our compartment that I stood in the doorway for a few moments near an open window. My companion was lying down in my berth. We still had nineteen hours of travel before us with no prospect of sleep, for sleep in those berths and over such a rough road was absolutely out of the question.

Near me (and spitting in the saddest manner out of the open window) stood the meek little American husband of the gray flannel and curl-papers, whose fury at my companion for her quick work with the customs officer knew no bounds.

The gray flannel had gone to bed again in the compartment

next to ours.

The precision of this gentleman's aim as he expectorated through the open window, and the marvellous rapidity with which he managed his diversion, led me to watch him. He looked tired and cold and ill. It was still dark outside, and the jolting of the train was almost unbearable. He had not once looked at me, but with his gaze still on the darkness he said, slowly,

"They can have the whole blamed country for all of me! *I* don't want it."

It was so exactly the way I felt that even though he said something worse than "blamed," I gave a shriek of delight, and my companion pounded the pillow in her cooperation of the sentiment.

"You are an American and you are Southern," I said.

"Yes'm. How did you know?"

"By your accent."

"Yes'm, I was born in Virginia. I was in the Southern army four years, and I love my country. I hate these blamed foreigners and their blamed churches and their infernal foreign languages. I am over here for my health, my wife says. But I have walked more miles in picture-galleries than I ever marched in the army. I've seen more pictures by Raphael than he could have painted if he'd 'a' had ten arms and painted a thousand years without stopping to eat or sleep. I've seen more 'old masters,' as they call 'em, but *I* call 'em *daubs*, all varnished till they are so slick that a fly would slip on 'em and break his neck. And the stone floors are so cold that I get cold clean up to my knees, and I don't get

　Lilian Bell

warm for a week. Yet I am over here for my health! Then the way they rob you—these blamed French! Lord, if I ever get back to America, where one price includes everything and your hotel bill isn't sent in on a ladder, and where I can keep warm, won't I just be *too* thankful."

Just then the gray-flannel door banged open and a hand reached out and jerked the poor little old man inside, and we heard him say, "But I was only blaming the French. I ain't happy over here." And a sharp voice said, "Well, you've said enough. Don't talk any more at all." Then she let him out again, but he did not find me in the corridor. He found his open window, and he leaned against our closed door and again aimed at the flying landscape, as he pondered over the disadvantages of Europe.

The sun was just rising over the cathedral as we reached Cologne.

"Let's get out here and have our breakfast comfortably, see the cathedral, and take the next train to Berlin," I said to my companion.

She is the courier and I am the banker. She hastily consulted her *indicateur* and assented. We only had about two seconds in which to decide.

"Let's throw these bags out of the window," she said. "I've seen other people do it, and the porters catch them."

"Don't *throw* them," I urged. "You will break my toilet bottles. Poke them out gently."

She did so, and we hopped off the train just at daybreak, perfectly delighted at doing something we had not planned.

A more lovely sight than the Cologne cathedral, with the rising sun gilding its numerous pinnacles and spires, would be difficult to imagine. The narrow streets were still comparatively dark, and when we arrived we heard the majestic notes of the organ in a Bach fugue, and found ourselves at early mass, with rows of humble worshippers kneeling before the high altar, and the twinkle of many candles in the soft gloom. As we stood and watched and listened, the smell of incense floated down to us, and gradually the first rays of the sun crept downward through the superb colored-glass windows and stained the marble statues in their niches into gorgeous hues of purple and scarlet and amber.

And as the priests intoned and the fresh young voices of an invisible choir floated out and the magnificent rumble of the organ shook the very foundation of the cathedral, we forgot that we were there to visit a sight of Cologne, we forgot our night of discomfort, we forgot everything but the spirit of worship, and we came away without speaking.

*   *   *   *   *

From Cologne to Dresden is stupid. We went through a country punctuated with myriads of tall chimneys of factories, which reminded us why so many things in England and America are stamped "Made in Germany."

We arrived at Dresden at five o'clock, and decided to stop there and go to the opera that night. The opera begins in Dresden at seven o'clock and closes at ten. The best seats are absurdly cheap, and whole families, whole schools, whole communities, I should say, were there together. I never saw so many children at an opera in my life. Coming straight from Paris, from the theatrical, vivacious, enthusiastic French audiences, with their abominable *claqueurs*, this first German audience seemed serious, thoughtful, appreciative, but unenthusiastic. They use more judgment about applause than the French. They never interrupt a scene or even a musical phrase with misplaced applause because the soprano has executed a flamboyant cadenza or the tenor has reached a higher note than usual. Their appreciation is slow but hearty and always worthily disposed. The French are given to exaggerating an emotion and to applauding an eccentricity. Even their subtlety is overdone.

The German drama is much cleaner than the French, the family tie is made more of, sentiment is encouraged instead of being ridiculed, as it too often is in America; but the German point of view of Americans is quite as much distorted as the French. That statement is severe, but true. For instance, it would be utterly impossible for the American girl to be more exquisitely misunderstood than by French and German men.

Berlin is so full of electric cars that it seemed much more familiar at first sight than Paris. It is a lovely city, although we ought to have seen it before Paris in order fully to appreciate it. Its Brandenburg Gate is most impressive, and I wanted to make some demonstration every time we drove under it and realized that the statue above it has been returned. Their statue of Victory in the Thiergarten is so hideous, however, that I was reminded of General Sherman's remark when he saw the Pension Office in Washington, "And they tell me the—thing is fireproof!"

The streets are filled with beautiful things, mostly German officers. The only trouble is that they themselves seem to know it only too well, and as they will not give us any of the sidewalk, we are obliged to admire them from the gutters. The only way you can keep Germans from knocking you into the middle of the street is to walk sideways and pretend you are examining the shop windows.

In the eyes of men, women are of little account in England compared to the way we are treated in America; of less in France; and of still less in Germany. We have not got to Russia yet.

Paris seems a city of leisure, Berlin a city of war. The streets of Paris are quite as full of soldiers as Berlin, but French soldiers look to me like mechanical toys. I have sent Billy a box of them for Christmas—of mechanical soldiers, I mean. The chief difference I noticed was that Billy's were smaller than the live ones, although French soldiers are small enough. That portion of the French army which I have seen—at Longchamps, Chalons-sur-Marne, Saumur, and at various other places—are, as a rule, undersized, badly dressed, and badly groomed. They do not look neat, nor even clean, if you want the truth. The uniform is very ugly, and was evidently designed for men thirteen feet high; so that on those comical little toy Frenchmen it is grotesque in the extreme.

Their trousers are always much too long, and so ample in width that they seem to need only a belt at the ankle to turn them into perfect Russian blouses. But English and German soldiers not only appear, but *are*, in perfect condition, as though they could go to war at a moment's notice, and would be glad of the chance.

I am keeping my eyes open to see how America bears comparison with other nations in all particulars. In point of appearance the English army stands first, the German second, the American third, and the French fourth. I put the American third only because our uniforms are less impressive. In everything else, except in numbers, they might easily stand first. But uniforms and gold lace, and bright scarlet and waving plumes, make a vast difference in appearance, and every country in the world recognizes this, except America. I wish that everybody in the United States who boasts of democracy and Jeffersonian simplicity could share my dissatisfaction in seeing our ambassadors at Court balls and diplomatic receptions in deacons' suits of modest black, without even a medal or decoration of any kind, except perhaps that gorgeous and overpowering insignia known as the Loyal Legion button, while every little twopenny kingdom of a mile square sends a representative in a uniform as brilliant as a peony and stiff with gold embroidery.

No matter how magnificent a man, personally, our ambassador may be, no matter how valuable his public services, no matter how unimpeachable his private character, I wish you could see how small and miserable and mean is the appearance he presents at Court functions, where every man there, except the representative of seventy millions of people, is in some sort of uniform. If it really were Thomas Jefferson whose administration inaugurated the disgusting simplicity which goes by his name, I wish the words had stuck in his throat and strangled him. "Jeffersonian simplicity!" How I despise it! Thomas Jefferson, I believe, was the first Populist. We had had gentlemen for Presidents before him, but he was the first one who rooted for votes with the common herd by catering to the gutter instead of to the skyline, and the tail end of his policy is to be seen in the mortifying appearance of our highest officials and representatives. *Hinc illae lachrymae!*

I looked at the servant who announced our names in Paris at General Porter's first official reception, and even he was much more gorgeous in dress than the master of the house, the Ambassador Extraordinary and Minister Plenipotentiary representing seventy millions of people! Not even in his uniform of a general! The only man in the room in plain black. The United States ought to treat her representatives better. When Mr. White at Berlin was received by the Emperor, he, too, was the only man in plain black.

No wonder we are taken no account of socially when we don't even give our ambassador a house, as all the other countries do, and when his salary is so inadequate. Every other ambassador except the American has a furnished house given him, and a salary sufficient to entertain as becomes the representative of a great country. All except *ours*! Yet none of them is obliged to entertain as continuously as our ambassador, because *only* Americans travel unremittingly, and *only* Americans expect their ambassador to be their host.

> "O wad some power the giftie gie us
> To see oursels as ithers see us!"

Of course I notice such things immensely more in Berlin than in Paris, because the glory of a Court is much more than the twinkle of a republic.

I have worked myself into such a towering rage over this subject that there is no getting down to earth gracefully or gradually. I have not polished off the matter by any manner of means. I have only just started in, but a row of stars will cool me off.

* * * * *

Before I came to Berlin I heard so much about Unter den Linden, that magnificent street of the city, that I could scarcely wait to get to it. I pictured it lined on both sides with magnificent linden-trees, gigantic, imposing, impressive. I had had no intimate acquaintance with linden-trees—and I wouldn't know one now if I should see it—but I had an idea from the name—linden, linden—that it was grand and waving; not so grand as an oak nor so waving as a willow,

Lilian Bell

but a cross between the two. I knew that I should see these great monarchs making a giant arch over this broad avenue and mingling their tossing branches overhead.

What I found when I arrived was a broad, handsome street. But those lindens! They are consumptive, stunted little saplings without sufficient energy to grow into real trees. They are set so far apart that you have time to forget one before you come to another, and as to their appearance—we have some just like them in Chicago where there is a leak in the gas-pipes near their roots.

On the day before Christmas we felt very low in our minds. We had the doleful prospect ahead of us of eating Christmas dinner alone in a strange country, and in a hotel at that, so we started out shopping. Not that we needed a thing, but it is our rule, "When you have the blues, go shopping." It always cures you to spend money.

Berlin shop-windows are much more fascinating even than those of Paris, because in Berlin there are so many more things that you can afford to buy that Paris seems expensive in comparison. We became so much interested in the Christmas display that we did not notice the flight of time. When we had bought several heavy things to weigh our trunks down a little more and to pay extra luggage on, I happened to glance at the sun, and it was just above the horizon. It looked to be about four o'clock in the afternoon, and we had had nothing to eat since nine o'clock, and even then only a cup of coffee. I felt myself suddenly grow faint and weak. "Heavens!" I said, "see what time it is! We have shopped all day and we have forgotten to get our luncheon."

My companion glanced at her watch.

"It's only half past eleven o'clock by my watch. I couldn't

have wound it last night. No, it is going."

"Perhaps the hands stick. They do on mine. Whenever I wind it, I have to hit it with the hair-brush to start it; and even then it loses time every day."

"Let's take them both to a jeweller," she said. "We can't travel with watches which act this way."

So we left them to be repaired, and as we came out, I said, "It will take us half an hour to get back to the hotel. Don't you think we ought to go in somewhere and get just a little something to sustain us?"

"Of course we ought," she said, in a weak voice. So we went in and got a light luncheon. Then we went back to the hotel, intending to lie down and rest after such an arduous day.

"We must not do this again," I said, firmly. "Mamma told me particularly not to overdo."

My companion did not answer. She was looking at the clock. It was just noon.

"Why, *that* clock has stopped too," she said.

But as we looked into the reading-room *that* clock struck twelve. Then it dawned on me, and I dropped into a chair and nearly had hysterics.

"It's because we are so far *north*!" I cried. "Our watches were all right and the sun's all right. That is as high as it can get!"

She was too much astonished to laugh.

"And you had to go in and get luncheon because you felt so

Lilian Bell

faint," she said, in a tone of gentle sarcasm.

"Well, you confessed to a fearful sense of goneness yourself."

"Don't tell anybody," she said.

"I should think not!" I retorted, with dignity. "I hope I have *some* pride."

"Have you presented your letter to the ambassador?" she asked.

"Yes, but it's so near Christmas that I suppose he won't bother about two waifs like us until after it's over."

"My! but you *are* blue," she said. "I never heard you refer to yourself as a waif before."

"I am a worm of the dust. I wish there wasn't such a thing as Christmas! I wonder what Billy will say when he sees his tree."

"You might cable and find out," she said. "It only costs about three marks a word. 'What did Billy say when he saw his tree?'—nine words—it would cost you about eight dollars, without counting the address."

Dead silence. I didn't think she was at all funny.

"Don't you think we ought to have champagne to-morrow?" she asked.

"What for? I hate the stuff. It makes me ill. Do *you* want it?"

"No, only I thought that, being Christmas, and very

expensive, perhaps it would do you good to spend—"

A knock on the door made us both jump.

"His Excellency the Ambassador of the United States to see the American ladies!"

It was, indeed, Mr. White and Mrs. White, and Lieutenant Allen, the Military Attache!

"Oh, those blessed angels!" I cried, buckling my belt and dashing for the wash-stand, thereby knocking the comb and hand-glass from the grasp of my companion.

They had come within an hour of the presentation of my letter, and they brought with them an invitation from Mrs. Allen for us to join them at Christmas dinner the next day, as Mrs. White said they could not bear to think of our dining alone.

I had many beautiful things done for me during my thirty thousand miles travel in Europe, but nothing stands out in my mind with more distinctness than the affectionate welcome I received into the homes of our representatives in Berlin. And, in passing, let me say this, I am distinctly proud of them, one and all. I say this because one hears many humiliating anecdotes of the mistakes made by the men and women sent to foreign Courts, appointed because they had earned some recognition for political services. Those of us who have strong national pride and a sense of the eternal fitness of things, are obliged to hear such things in shamed silence, and offer no retort, for there can be no possible excuse for mortifying lapses of etiquette. And these things will continue until our government establishes a school of diplomacy and makes a diplomatic career possible to a man.

As long as it is possible for an ex-coroner or sheriff to be appointed to a secretaryship of a foreign legation—a man who does not speak the language and whose wife understands better how to cope with croup and measles than with wives of foreign diplomats who have been properly trained for this vocation, just so long shall we be obliged to bear the ridicule heaped upon us over here, which our government never hears, and wouldn't care if it did!

Imagine the relief with which I met our Berlin representatives! At the end of four years there will be no sly anecdotes whispered behind fans at *their* expense, for they have all held the same office before and are well equipped by training, education, and native tact to bear themselves with a proud front at one of the most difficult Courts of Europe. I look back upon that little group of Americans with feelings of unmixed pride.

Mr. White invited us to go with him that afternoon to see the tombs of the kings at Charlottenburg; and when his gorgeous-liveried footman came to announce his presence, the hotel proprietor and about forty of his menials nearly crawled on their hands and knees before us, so great is their deference to pomp and power.

I wish to associate Berlin with this beautiful mausoleum. It is circular in shape, and the light falls from above through lovely colored-glass windows upon those recumbent marble statues. The dignity, the still, solemn beauty of those pale figures lying there in their eternal repose, fill the soul with a sense of the great majesty of death.

When we got back to the hotel we found that the same good fortune which had attended us so far had ordained that the American mail should arrive that day, and behold! there were all our Christmas letters timed as accurately as if they had only gone from Chicago to New York.

Christmas letters! How they go to the heart when one is five thousand miles away! How we tore up to our rooms, and oh! how long it seemed to get the doors unlocked and the electric light turned up, and to plant ourselves in the middle of the bed to read and laugh and cry and interrupt each other, and to read out paragraphs of Billy's funny baby-talk!

While we were still discussing them, the proprietor came up to announce to us that there was to be a Christmas Eve entertainment in the main dining-room that evening, and would the American ladies do him the honor to come down? The American ladies would.

When we went down we found that the enormous dining-room was packed with people, all standing around a table which ran around two sides of the room. A row of Christmas trees, covered with cotton to represent snow, occupied the middle of the room, and at one end was a space reserved for the lady guests, and in each chair was a handsome bouquet of violets and lilies-of-the-valley.

This entertainment was for the servants of the hotel, of whom there were three hundred and fifty.

First they sang a Lutheran hymn, very slowly, as if it were a dirge. Then there was a short sermon. Then another hymn. Then the manager made a little speech and called, for three cheers for the proprietor, and they gave them with a fervor that nearly split the ears of the groundlings.

Then a signal was given, and in less than one minute three hundred and fifty paper bags were produced, and three hundred and fifty plates full of oranges, apples, buns, and sweetened breads were emptied into them. The table looked as if a plague of grasshoppers had swept over it.

Then each servant presented a number and received a present from the tree, and that ended the festivity. But so typical of the fatherland, so paternal, so like one great family!

Participating in this simple festival brought a little of the Christmas feeling home to us and made us almost happy. We knew that our American parcels would not be delivered until the next day, so we had but just time to reread our precious letters when the clock struck twelve, and with much solemnity my companion and I presented each other with our modest Christmas present—which each had announced that she wanted and had helped to select! But, then, who would not rather select one's own Christmas presents, and so be sure of getting things that one wants?

On Christmas morning registered packages began to arrive for both of us. The first ten presents to arrive for my companion were pocket-handkerchiefs. My first ten were all books. Evidently the dear family had thought that American books would be most acceptable over here, and I could see, with a feeling that warmed my heart, how carefully they had consulted my taste, and had tried to remember to send those I wanted. But I am of a frugal mind, and thoughts of the extra luggage to be paid on bound books would intrude themselves. However, I made no remark over the first ten, but before the day was over I had received twenty-two books and one pen-wiper, and my vocabulary was exhausted. My companion continued to receive handkerchiefs until the room was full of them. Take it all together, there was a good deal of sameness about our presents, but they have been useful as dinner anecdotes ever since. Now that I have sent all mine to be stored at Munroe's, together with all my other necessities, I feel lighter and more buoyant both in mind and trunk.

A Christmas dinner in a foreign land, in the midst of the diplomatic corps, is the most undiplomatic thing in the world, for that is the one time when you can cease to be diplomatic and dare to criticise the government and make personal remarks to your heart's content.

It was a beautiful dinner, and after it was over we were all invited to the children's entertainment at Mrs. Squiers's. She had gathered about fifty of the American colony for Christmas carols and a tree. Immediately after the ambassador arrived the children marched in and recited in chorus the verses about the birth of Christ, beginning, "Now in the days of Herod the King." Then they sang their carols, and then "Stille Nacht," and they sang them beautifully, in their sweet, childish voices.

After these exercises the doors were thrown open, and the most beautiful Christmas-tree I ever beheld burst upon the view of those children, who nearly went wild with delight.

After everybody had gone home except "the diplomatic family," which for the time being included us, we picnicked on the remains of the Christmas turkey for supper, and there was as little ceremony about it as if it had been at an army post on the frontier. We had a beautiful time, and everybody seemed to like everybody very much and to be excellent friends.

Then Mr. and Mrs. White escorted us back to our hotel, which wasn't at all necessary, but which illustrates the way in which they treated us all the time we were there.

This ended a truly beautiful Christmas, for, aside from being unexpected and in striking contrast to the forlornness we had anticipated, we had been taken into the families of beautiful people, whose home life was an honor and an inspiration to share.

On New Year's day we started early and went to Potsdam to visit the palace of Sans Souci.

A most curious and interesting little old man who had been a guide there for thirty years showed us through the grounds, where the King's greyhounds are buried, and where he pleaded to be buried with them. The guide had no idea that he possessed a certain dramatic genius for pathos, for, parrot-like, he was repeating the story he had told perhaps a thousand times before. But when he showed us the graves of the greyhounds which ate the poisoned food which had been prepared for the King, he said:

"And they lie here. Not there with the other dogs, the favorites of the King, but here, alone, disgraced, without even a headstone. Without even their names, although they saved the great King from death and gave their lives for his. Yet they lie here, and the others lie there. It is the way of the world, ladies."

Then he took us to the top of the terrace facing the palace, and, pointing to the entrance, he said:

"In the left wing were the chambers of the King's guests. In the right wing were his own. Therefore, he placed a comma between those two words 'Sans' and 'Souci,' to indicate that those at the left were 'without,' while with himself was— 'Care.'"

While we were there the Emperor drove by and spoke to our cabman, saying, "How is business?" Seeing how much pleasure it gave the poor fellow to repeat it, we kept asking him to tell vis what the Kaiser said to him.

First my companion would say:

"When was it and what happened?"

And when he had quite finished, I would say:

"It wasn't the Emperor himself, was it? It must have been the coachman who spoke to you."

"No, not so, ladies. It was the great Kaiser himself. He said to me—" And then we would get the whole thing over again. It was charming to see his pleasure.

When we returned home we entered the hotel between rows of palms, and we dropped money into each of them. It seemed to me that fifty servants were between me and the elevators. However, it was New Year's, and we tried not to be bored by it.

People talk so much of the expense of foreign travel, but to my mind the greatest expenditures are in paying for extra luggage and in fees. Otherwise, I fancy that travel is much the same if one travels luxuriously, and that in the long run things would be about equal. The great difference is that in America all travel luxuries are given to you for the price of your ticket, and here you pay for each separate necessity, to say nothing of luxury, and your ticket only permits you to breathe. But the annoyance of this continuous habit of feeing makes life a burden. One pays for everything. It is the custom of the country, and no matter if you arrange to have "service included," it is in the air, in the eyes of the servants, in the whole mental atmosphere, and you fee, you fee, you fee until you are nearly dead from the bother of it. In Germany they raise their hats and rise to their feet every time you pass, even if you pass every seven minutes, and when the time comes for you to go, you have to pay for the wear and tear of these hats.

In Paris, at the theatre, you fee the woman who shows you to your seat, you fee the woman who opens the door and the woman who takes your wraps. One night in midsummer we stepped across from the Grand Hotel to the opera without even a scarf for a wrap, and the woman was so disappointed that we were handed from one attendant to another some half dozen times as "three ladies without wraps." And the next one would look us over from head to foot and repeat the words, "Three ladies without wraps," until we laughed in their faces.

French servants are the cleverest in the world if you want versatility, but they are absolutely shameless in their greed, and look at the size of your coin before they thank you. In fact, the words in which they thank you indicate whether your fee was not enough, only modest, or handsome.

"It is not too much, madam," or "thanks, madam," or "I thank you a thousand times" show your status in their estimation.

If you are an American they reserve the right to rob you by the impudence of their demands, until rather than have a scene, you give them all they ask. I have followed in the footsteps of a French woman and given exactly what she did, and had my money flung in derision upon the pavement.

German servants seem to have more self-respect, for while they expect it quite as much, they smile and thank you and never look at the coin before your eyes. Perhaps they know from the feeling of it, but even if you place it upon the table behind them they thank you and never look at it or take it until you turn away.

However, you fee unmercifully here too. You fee the man at

the bank who cashes your checks, you fee the street-car conductor who takes your fare, you fee every uniformed hireling of the government, whether he has done anything for you or not.

The only persons whom I have neglected to fee so far are the ambassadors.

But then, they do not wear uniforms!

IV

ON BOARD THE YACHT "HELA"

I am just able to sit up, and I couldn't think of a thing I wanted to eat if I thought a week. I came on this yachting trip because my friends begged me to. They said it would be an experience for me. It has been.

The *Hela* started out with a party of ten on board, who were on pleasure bent. We have come up the English Channel from Dinard to Ostend, but before we had been out an hour we struck a gale, to which veterans on seasickness will refer for many a long day as "that fearful time on the Channel."

On the whole, I don't know but that I myself might be considered a veteran on seasickness. I have averaged crossing the Channel once a month ever since I've been over here. I have got into the habit of crossing the Channel, and I can't seem to stop. It always appears that I am in the wrong place for whatever is going on, for just as sure as I go to London somebody sends for me to come to Paris, and I rush for the Channel, and I have no sooner unpacked my trunks in Paris, and bargained that service and electric lights shall be included, than somebody discovers that I am imperatively needed in England, and I make for the Channel again. The Channel is like Jordan. It always rolls between.

But even in crossing the Channel there is everything in knowing how. I have discarded the private state-room. It is too expensive, and I am not a bit less uncomfortable than when occupying six feet of the settee in the ladies' cabin, with my feet in the flowers of another woman's hat. In fact, I prefer the latter. The other woman is always too ill to protest or to move. I have now, by long and patient practice, proved to my own satisfaction what serves me best in case of seasickness. I will not stay on deck. I will not eat or drink anything to cure it. I will not take anything to prevent it. I will not sit up, and I will not keep my hat on. When I go on board of a Channel steamer my first act is to shake hands with my friends and to go below. There I present the stewardess with a modest testimonial of my regard. I also give her my ticket. Then I select the most desirable portion of the settee, near a port-hole, from which I can get fresh air. I take off my hat and lie down. The steamer may not start for an hour. No matter. There I am, and there I stay. The Channel may be as smooth as glass, but I travel better flat. Like manuscript, I am not to be rolled. Sometimes I am not ill at all, but I freely confess that those times are infrequent and disappointing.

Now, of course, this is always to be expected in crossing the Channel, but my friends said in going up the Channel we would not get those choppy waves, and that I would find that the *Hela* swam like a duck.

In analyzing that statement since, with a view to classifying it as truth or otherwise, I have studied my recollections of ducks, and I have come to the conclusion that in a rough sea a duck has every right to be seasick, for she wobbles like everything else that floats. For real comfort, give me something that's anchored. Nevertheless, I was persuaded to join the party.

Everybody came down at Dinard to see us off, and quite a number even went over to St. Malo with us in the electric launch, for the *Hela* drew too much water to enter the harbor at Dinard at low tide.

We were a merry party for the first hour on board the *Hela*— until we struck the gale. It has seemed to me since that our evil genius was hovering over us from the first, and simply waited until it would be out of the question to turn back before emptying the vials of her wrath on our devoted heads. It did not rain. The sun kept a malevolent eye upon us all the time. It simply blew just one straight, unrelenting, unswerving gale. And it came so suddenly. We were all sitting on deck as happy as angels, when, without a word of warning, the *Hela* simply turned over on her side and threw us all out of our chairs. I caught at a mast as I went by and clung like a limpet. There was tar on the mast. It isn't there any more. It is on the front of my new white serge yachting dress. Jimmie coasted across the deck, and landed on his hands and knees against the gunwale. If he had persisted in standing up he would have gone overboard. The women all shrieked and remained in a tangled heap of chairs, and rugs, and petticoats, waiting for the yacht to right herself, and for the men to come and pick them up. But the yacht showed no intention of righting herself. She continued to careen in the position of a cab going round Piccadilly Circus on one wheel. The sailors were all running around like ants on an ant-hill, and the captain was shouting orders, and even lending a hand with the ropes himself. I don't know the nautical terms, but they were taking down the middle sail— the mainsail, that's it. It did not look dangerous, because the sun kept shining, and I never thought of being frightened. I just clung to the mast, watching the other people right themselves, and laughing, when suddenly everything ceased to be funny. The decks of the *Hela* took on a wavy motion, and I blinked my eyes in order to see better, for everything was getting very indistinct, and there were green spots on the sun. Suddenly I realized that I was a long way from home, and that I was even a long way from my state-room. I only had just about sense enough left to remember that the mast was my very best friend and that I must cling there.

After that, I remember that somebody came up behind me and pried my hands loose from the mast.

The doctor's voice said, "Can you walk?"

I smiled feebly and said, "I used to know how." But evidently my efforts were not highly successful, for he picked me up, white serge, tar, green spots on the sun, and all, and carried me below, a limp and humiliated bit of humanity.

Mrs. Jimmie and Commodore Strossi followed with more anxiety than the occasion warranted.

Then Mrs. Jimmie sent the men away, and I felt pillows under my head, and camphor under my nose, and hot-water bags about me; and I must have gone to sleep or died, or something, for I don't remember anything more until the next day.

They were very nice to me, for I was such a cheerful invalid. It seemed to surprise them that I could even pretend to be happy. I knew that it must be an uncommon gale from the way Commodore Strossi studied the charts, and because even his wife, for whom the yacht was named, was ill, and she had spent half her life on the sea. The poor little French cabin-boy was ill, too, and went around, with a Nile-green countenance, waiting on people, before he was obliged to retire from active service.

The pitching of the yacht was something so terrible that it got to be hysterically funny. It couldn't seem dangerous with the sun streaming down the companion-way and past my state-room windows. About five o'clock on the second day they began to tack, and then I heard shrieks of laughter and the crash of china, and groans from the saloon settee, where young Bashforth was lying ghastly ill.

At the first lurch my trunk tipped over, and all the bottles on the wash-stand bounded across to the bed, and most of them struck me on the head. It frightened me so that I shrieked, and Jimmie came running down to see if I was killed.

As I raised my head I saw his horrified gaze fairly riveted to my face, and I felt something softly trickling down. I touched it, and then looked at my hand and discovered that it was wet and red.

"Good heavens, your face is all cut open," gasped Jimmie, in a voice that revealed his terror.

Mrs. Jimmie was just behind him, and I saw her turn pale. In a flash I saw myself disfigured for life, and probably having to be sewed up. The pain in my face became excruciating, and I began to think yachting rather serious business.

"Run for the doctor, Jimmie," said his wife. Jimmie obediently ran.

"Does it hurt very much, dear?" she said, sitting on the edge of the bed.

"Awfully," I murmured.

The doctor came, followed by Francois, with a basin of hot water and sponges, and a nasty-looking little case of instruments. Mrs. Jimmie held my hand. They turned on the electric lights and opened the windows. Jimmie had my salts. The doctor carefully wet a sponge and tenderly bathed my cheek, and I held my breath ready to shriek if he hurt me. Commodore Strossi stood at the door with an anxious face. Suddenly the doctor reached for a broken bottle half hidden under my pillow.

"Oh, what is it, doctor?" asked Mrs. Jimmie. "What makes you look so queer?"

"This is iodine on her face. Her bottle has emptied itself. That is all."

We gazed at each other for a moment or two, then I nearly went into hysterics. Jimmie's face was a study.

"You said it was blood, Jimmie," I said.

"Well, you said it hurt," he retorted.

"Well, it did. When you said I was covered with blood it hurt awfully."

The doctor went out much chagrined that he had not been called upon to sew up a wound. I had a relapse, brought on by young Bashforth's jeering remarks as he frantically clung to the handles of the locker which formed the back of the settee where he lay prostrate.

I was too utterly done up to reply, for two days' violent seasickness rather takes the mental ginger out of one's make-up. But Fate avenged me in this wise. The door of my state-room opened into the dining-room, and my bed faced the door. Opposite to me was the settee on which Bashforth was coiled, and back of him was the locker for the tinned mushrooms, sardines, lobster, shrimp, caviar, deviled ham, and all the things which well people can eat. This locker had brass handles let into the mahogany, and to these handles the poor fellow clung when the yacht lurched.

His cruel words of derision had hardly left his pale lips before they tacked again. He was not holding on, but he hastily snatched at the handles. He was too late, however, for he was tossed from the settee to the legs of the dining-room table (which, fortunately, were anchored) without touching the floor at all. He described a perfect parabola. It was just the way I should have tossed him had I been Destiny. He gripped the table-legs like a vise, coiling himself around them like a poor navy-blue python with a green face. He thought the worst was over, but in his last clutch at the locker he had accidentally opened it, and at the next lurch of the yacht all the cans bounded out and battered his unprotected back like a shower of grape-shot. The yacht lurched again and the cans rolled back. She pitched forward, and again the mushrooms and deviled ham aimed for him. The noise brought everybody, and at first nobody tried to help him. They just couldn't see because of the tears in their eyes from laughing. As for me, I managed to crawl to the foot of the bed and cling to a post, so weak I couldn't wipe the tears away, but laying up an amount of enjoyment which will enrich my old age.

Finally, Jimmie got sorry for him, and went and tried to pick him up. But he was laughing so, he dropped him.

"Oh, Jimmie," I pleaded. "Don't drop anybody who is seasick. Drop well people if you must. But put him on the settee carefully."

"I'll put him there," said Jimmie, wiping his eyes on his coat-sleeve. "But I don't say I'll do it the first time I try. I'll get him there by dinner-time—I hope."

It was dangerous to ridicule anybody in that gale, for the doctor in the companion-way was leaning in at my window and laughing in his big English voice, when the *Hela* lurched and pitched him half-way into my state-room. There he balanced with his hands on my trunk.

He was rather a tight fit, which interested Jimmie more than young Bashforth, so he left the boy and came around and pried the doctor back into the companion-way.

The *Hela* was a fickle jade, for no sooner would she shake us up in such an alarming manner than she would seem to regret her violence, and would skim like a bird for an hour or so, with no perceptible motion. She would not even flap her big white wings, but she cut through the water with a whir and a rush which exhilarated me as flying must stir the heart of a sea-gull.

She behaved so well after five o'clock that they decided to try to eat dinner from the dinner-table—a thing they had not done since we started. There were only four of them able to appear—Mr. and Mrs. Jimmie, the doctor, and the Commodore.

They put the racks up and took every precaution. The only mistake they made was in using the yacht's lovely china, which bore the Strossi crest under the *Hela's* private flag.

Jimmie and his wife sat opposite each other. I put three pillows under my head, the better to watch them, when suddenly the yacht tilted Mrs. Jimmie and her chair over backward. Jimmie saw her going and reached to save her. But he forgot to set down his soup-plate. The result was that she got Jimmie's soup in her face, and that he slid clear across the table on his hands and knees, taking china and table-cloth with him, and they all landed on top of poor Mrs. Jimmie (who, even as I write, is in her stateroom having her hair washed).

Her chief wail, when she could speak, was not that her head ached from the blow, or that she was half strangled with tepid soup, but that Jimmie had broken all the china. She could not be comforted until the Commodore proved that some of the china had been broken previously, by showing her the fragments wrecked on the first day out.

That last catastrophe has apparently settled things. Everybody has turned in to repair damages, and, perhaps, afterwards to sleep.

The Commodore is studying the charts on the dining-room table, and the captain, an American, has just put his head in at the door and said:

"She's sailing twelve knots an hour under just the fores'l, sir, and she's running like a scairt dog."

* * * * *

Americans are so accustomed to outrageous distances that a journey of fifty hours is mere play. But I sincerely believe that no other trait of ours causes the European to regard our nation with such suspicion as our utter unconcern of long journeys. Nothing short of accession to a title or to escape being caught by the police would induce the Continental to travel over a few hours. So when I decided to go to Poland in order to be a member of a gorgeous house-party, I might as well have robbed a bank and given my friends something to be suspicious of. They never believed that I would do such a fatiguing and unheard-of thing until I really left.

But Poland has always beckoned me like a friend—a friend which combined all the poetry, romance, fascination, nobility, and honor of a first love. If the Pole is proud, he has something to be proud of. His honor has dignity. His country's sorrows touch the heart. Polish literature has sentiment, her music has fire, her men of genius stand out like heroes, her women are adorable. Balzac describes not only one but a not infrequent type when he dedicates *Modeste Mignon* "To a Polish Lady" in the most exquisite apostrophe which ever graced the entrance-hall to one of the noblest novels of this inimitable master.

"Daughter of an enslaved land, angel through love, witch through fancy, child by faith, aged by experience, man in brain, woman in heart, giant by hope, mother through sorrow, poet in thy dreams, to Thee belongs this book, in which thy love, thy fancy, thy experience, thy sorrow, thy hope, thy dreams, are the warp through which is shot a woof less brilliant than the poesy of thy soul, whose expression when it shines upon thy countenance is, to those who love thee, what the characters of a lost language are to scholars."

Such a tribute as this would of itself be sufficient to turn the heart expectantly towards Poland, to say nothing of the interest her history has for the brain. The history of Poland is one long struggle for home and country. The Pole is a patriot by inheritance. His patriotism, goes deeper than his love.

His country comes first in his soul, and for that reason the Poles have in me an enthusiastic ally, an ardent admirer, and a sympathetic friend.

In speaking of the story of Poland with a cold-blooded reader of history I expressed my appreciation of the noble proportions of their struggles and my sympathy for their present unfortunate plight, to which she replied: "Yes, but it is so entirely their own fault. They are so fiery, so precipitate, so romantic. They got *themselves* into it! Their poesy and romance and folly make them charming as individuals, but ridiculous as a nation. I like the Poles, but I have no patience with Poland." How exactly the world's verdict on the artistic temperament! There is a round hole, and, lo and behold! all squares must be forced into it!

Suppose that everything resolved itself into the commonplace; where would be your imagination, your fancy, your rich experience of the heart and soul? Poland furnishes just this element in history. Her struggles are so romantic, her follies so charmingly natural to a high-strung nation, her despair so profound, her frequent revolutions so buoyant in hope, that she reminds me of a brilliant woman striving to make dull women understand her, and failing as persistently and completely as the artistic temperament always fails.

A frog spat at a glowworm. "Why do you spit at me?" said the glowworm. "Why do you shine so?" said the frog.

Poland's singers have voices so piercingly sweet; her novelists have pens touched with such divine fire; her actors portray so much of the soul; her patriots have always shown such reckless and inspiring bravery; and now, in her desolation and subjection, there is still so much pride, such noble dignity under her losses, that of all the countries in the world Poland holds both the heart and mind by a fascination of which she herself is unconscious, marking a noble simplicity of soul which is in itself an added indication of her queenly inheritance.

Julia Marlowe in her *Countess Valeska* is a Pole to her finger-tips. Her acting is superb. Cleopatra herself never felt nor inspired a diviner passion than Valeska; but when it came to a question of her love or her country she rose above self with an almost superhuman effort and saved her country at the expense of her love.

No American who has not the same awful passion of patriotism; no one who is not a lover of his country above home or friends or wife or children; who does not love his America second only to his God; whose blood does not prickle in his veins at the sound of "The Star-Spangled Banner," and whose eyes do not fill with tears at the sight of "Old Glory" floating anywhere, can understand of what patriotism the Pole is capable.

Nor can one who has not the foolish, romantic, nervous, high-strung, artistic temperament understand from within Poland's national history. For that reason one is apt to find famous places in Europe which have only an historical significance somewhat disappointing. One fails to find in a battle fought for the sake of conquest by an overweening ambition such soul-stirring pathos as in the leading of a forlorn hope from the spirit of patriotism, or of a woman's pleadings where a man's arguments have failed. For that reason Austerlitz touches one not so nearly as the struggle around Memel. As we drew near Memel things began to look lonely and foreign and queer, and its picturesque features were enhanced by recollection of Napoleon and Queen Louise.

Memel is near Tilsit, and the river Niemen, or Memel, empties into the Baltic just below here. The conference on the raft appeals to me as one of the most thrilling and yet pitiably human events in all history.

Its sickening anticlimax to poor Queen Louise was so exactly in keeping with the smaller disappointments which assail her more humble sister women in every walk of life that it takes on the air of a heart tragedy. I tried to imagine the feelings of the Queen when *she* journeyed to Memel to hold her famous interview with Napoleon. How her pride must have suffered at the thought of lowering herself to plead for her husband and her country at Napoleon's hands! How she hated him before she saw him! How she more than hated him after she left him! How she must have scorned the beauty upon which Napoleon commented so idly when a nation's honor was at stake! A typical act of the emperor of the French nation! Napoleon proved by that one episode that he was more French than Corsican.

In the Queen's illness at Memel she was so poorly housed that long lines of snow sifted in through the roof and fell across her bed. But that was as nothing to her mental disquiet while the fate of her beloved Prussia hung in the balance.

There is a bridge across the Memel at the exact spot where the famous raft conference is said to have taken place. As we crossed this bridge it seemed so far removed from those stormy days of strife that it was difficult to imagine the magnificent spectacle of the immense armies of Napoleon and Alexander drawn up on either bank, while these two powerful monarchs were rowed out to the raft to decide the fate of Frederick William and his lovely queen.

And although to them Prussia was the issue of the hour, how like the history of individual lives was this conference! For Prussia's fate was almost ignored, while the conversation originally intended to consume but a few moments lengthened into hours, and Napoleon and Alexander, having sworn eternal friendship, proceeded to divide up Europe between them, and parted with mutual expressions of esteem and admiration, having quite forgotten a trifle like the King and Queen of Prussia and their rage of anxiety.

But all these memories of Napoleon and Prussia gave way

before the vital fact that we were to visit a lovely Polish princess and see some of her charming home life. I had been duly informed by my friends of the various ceremonies which I would encounter, and which, I must confess, rendered me rather timid. I only hoped my wits would not desert me at the crucial moment.

For instance, if the archbishop were there I must give him my hand and then lean forward and kiss his sleeve just below the shoulder. I only hoped my chattering teeth would not meet in his robe. So when I saw the state carriage of the princess at the station of Memel, drawn by four horses, and with numbers of servants in such queer liveries to attend to my luggage, I simply breathed a prayer that I would get through it all successfully; and if not, that they would lay any lapses at the door of my own eccentricities, and not to the ignorance of Americans in general, for I never wish to disgrace my native land.

The servants wore an odd flat cap, like a tam-o'-shanter with a visor. Their coats were of bright blue, with the coat-of-arms of the princess on the brass buttons. This coat reached nearly to their feet, and in the back it was gathered full and stiffened with canvas, for all the world like a woman's pannier. I thought I should die the first time I got a side view of those men.

It was late Friday afternoon when we left the train, and we drove at a tremendous pace through lonely forests which we were only too happy to leave behind us. Suddenly we came upon the little village of Kretynga, whose streets were paved with cobblestones the size of a man's two fists.

To drive slowly over cobblestones is not a joy, but to drive four Russian horses at a gallop over such cobblestones as those was something to make you bite your tongue and to break your teeth and to shake your very soul from its socket.

The town is inhabited by Polish Jews, and a filthy, greasy, nauseating set they are, both men and women. The men wear two or three long, oily, tight curls in front of their ears. Their noses are hooked like a parrot's. Their countenances are sinister, and I believe they have not washed since the Flood. The women, when they marry, shave their heads. Then they either wear huge wigs, which they use to wipe their hands on without the ceremony of washing them first, or else they wear a black or white or gray satin hood-piece with a line to imitate the parting of the hair embroidered on it.

Nothing is clean about them. I no longer wonder that Jews are expelled from Russia. It makes one rather respect Russia as a clean country. As it was Friday night, one window-sill in each house was filled with a row of lighted candles representing each member of the family who was either absent or dead.

Being so far away from home myself, this appealed to me as such a touching custom that it made my eyes smart.

Presently a clearing in the forest revealed the famous monastery of Kretynga—a monastery famous for being peopled with priests and monks whom the Tzar has exiled because they took too much interest in politics for his nerves. Then soon after passing this monastery we entered the grounds of the castle. Still the longest part of the drive lay before us, for this one of the many estates of the Princess lies between the Memel and the Baltic Sea, and covers a large territory.

But finally, after driving through an avenue of trees which are worth a dictionary of words all to themselves, we came to the castle, a huge structure, which seemed to spread out before us interminably, for it was too dark to see anything but its majestic outlines.

The Princess in her own home was even lovelier than she had been in Paris, and charitably allowed us to have one night's rest before meeting the family.

About three o'clock in the morning I was awakened by a mournful chant, all in minor, which began beneath my windows and receded, growing fainter and fainter, until at last it died away. It was the hymn which the peasants always sing as they go forth to their work in the fields; but its mournful cadence haunted me. The next morning the largeness of the situation dawned upon me. The size of the rooms and their majestic furnishings were almost barbaric in their splendor. The tray upon which my breakfast was served was of massive silver. The coffee-pot, sugar-bowl, and plates were of repousse silver, exquisitely wrought, but so large that one could hardly lift them.

In a great openwork basket of silver were any number of sweetened breads and small cakes and buns, all made by the baker in the castle, who all day long does nothing but bake bread and pastry. They do not serve hot milk with coffee, for which I blessed them from the bottom of my soul, but they have little brown porcelain jugs which they fill with cream so thick that you have to take it out with a spoon—it won't pour,—and these they heat in ovens, and so serve you hot cream for your coffee.

I call the gods from Olympus to testify to the quality of the nectar this combination produces. Some of those little porcelain jugs are going on their travels soon.

Meeting the various members of the Princess's charming family and remembering their titles was not an ordeal at all—at least it was not after it was over. They were quite like other people, except that their manners were unusually good. There was to be a hunt that morning—an amusing, luxurious sort of hunt quite in my line; one where I could go in a carriage and see the animals caught, but where I need not see them killed.

They were to hunt a mischievous little burrowing animal something like our badger, which is as great a pest to Poland as the rabbits are to Australia. They destroy the crops by eating their roots, so every little while a hunt is organized to destroy them in large numbers. The foresters had been sent out the night before to discover a favorite haunt of theirs, and to fill up all the entrances to their burrows; so all that we had to do was to drive to the scene of action.

It sounds simple enough, but I most solemnly assure you that it was anything but a simple drive to one fresh from the asphalt of Paris, for, like Jehu, they drove furiously.

Their horses are all wild, runaway beasts, and they drive them at an uneven gallop resembling the gait of our fire-engine horses at home, except that ours go more slowly. Sometimes the horses fall down when they drive across country, as they stop only for stone walls or moats. The carriages must be built of iron, for the front wheels drop a few feet into a burrow every now and then, and at such times an unwary American is liable to be pitched over the coachman's head. "Hold on with both hands, shut your eyes, and keep your tongue from between your teeth," would be my instructions to one about to "take a drive" in Poland.

When we came to the place we found the foresters watching the *dachshunde*. These I discovered to be long, flat, shallow dogs with stumpy legs—a dog which an American has described as "looking as if he was always coming out from under a bureau." Very cautiously here and there the foresters uncovered a burrow, and a *dachshund* disappeared. Then from below ground came the sounds of fighting. The *dachshunde* had found their prey. The foresters ran about, stooping to locate the sound. When they discovered the spot a dozen of them at once began to dig as fast as they could.

Presently a writhing, rolling, barking bunch of fur and flying sand came into view, when a forester with a long forked stick caught the animal just back of its head and flung it into a coarse sack, which was then tied up and thrown aside, and the hunt went on. After we all went home the foresters gathered up these bags and killed the poor little animals somehow—mercifully, I hope.

The dinner, which came at two o'clock, was so much of a function, on account of the number of guests in the house, that it impressed itself upon my memory.

First in the salon there were small tables set, containing *hors d'oeuvres*. There were large decanters containing *vodke*, a liquor something like Chinese rice-brandy. There were smoked goose, smoked bear, and salmon, white and black bread, all sorts of sausages, anchovies and caviar, of course. After these had been tasted largely by the guests who were not Americans, and who knew that a formidable dinner yet had to be discussed, we were all seated at a table in the grand dining-room.

There were a hundred of us, and the table held enough for twice that many. We began with a hot soup made of fermented beet-juice. This we found to be delicious, but I seemed to be eating transparent red ink with parsley in it. This was followed by a cold soup made of sour cream and cucumbers, with *ecrevisse*, a small and delicious lobster. There was ice in this.

Cucumbers and sour cream! Let me see, wasn't it President Taylor who died of eating cherries and milk?

Then came a salad of chicken and lettuce, and then huge roasts garnished with exquisite French skill.

After the sweets came the fruit, such fruits as even our own California cannot produce, with white raspberries of a size and taste quite indescribable. When dinner is over comes a very pretty custom. The hostess, whose seat is nearest the door, rises, and each guest kisses her hand or her arm as he passes out, and thanks her in a phrase for her hospitality. Sometimes it is only "Thank you, princess"; sometimes "Many thanks for your beautiful dinner," or anything you like. They speak Polish to each other and to their servants, but they are such wonderful linguists that they always address a guest in his own language. To their peasants, however, who speak an unlearnable dialect, they are obliged always to have an interpreter.

At six o'clock came tea from samovars four feet high and of the most gorgeous repousse silver. Melons, fruit, and all sorts of bread are served with this. Then at eight a supper, very heavy, very sumptuous, very luxurious.

The whole day had been charming, exhilarating, different from anything we had ever seen before; but there was to follow something which impressed itself upon my excitable nerves with a fascination so bewildering that I can think of but one thing which would give me the same amount of heavenly satisfaction. This would be to have Theodore Thomas conduct the Chicago orchestra in the "Tannhaeuser" overture in the Court of Honor at the World's Fair some night with a full moon.

But to return. The Princess excused herself to her Protestant guests after supper, and then her family, with the servants and all the guests who wished, assembled in the winter garden to sing hymns to the Virgin. The winter garden is like a gigantic conservatory four stories high. It connects the two wings of the castle on the ground floor, and all the windows and galleries of the floors above overlook it.

It is the most beautiful spot even in the daytime that I ever saw connected with any house built for man. But at night to look down upon its beauty, with its palms, its tall ferns, its growing, climbing, waving vines and flowering shrubs, with its divine odors and fragrances and sweet dampnesses from mosses and lovely, moist, green, growing things, is to have one's soul filled with a poetry undreamed of on the written page.

The candles dotting the soft gloom, the spray from the fountains blowing in the air and tinkling into their marble basins, the tones of the grand organ rumbling and soaring up to us, the moonlight pouring through the great glass dome and filtering through the waving green leaves, dimpling on the marble statues and making trembling shades and shadows upon the earnest faces of the worshippers, the penetrating sadness of their minor hymns—all the sights and sounds and fragrances of this winter garden made of that hour "one to be forever marked with a white stone."

V

VILNA, RUSSIA

We met our first real discourtesy in Berlin at the hands of a German, and although he was only the manager of an hotel, we lay it up against him and cannot forgive him for it. It happened in this wise:

My companion, being the courier, bought our tickets straight through to St. Petersburg, with the privilege of stopping a week in Vilna, where we were to be the guests of a Polish nobleman. When she sent the porter to check our trunks she told him in faultless German to check them only to Vilna on those tickets. But as her faultless German generally brings us soap when she orders coffee, and hot water when she calls for ice, I am not so severe upon the stupidity of the porter as she is. However, when he came back and asked for fifty-five marks extra luggage to St. Petersburg we gave a wail, and explained to the manager, who spoke English, that we were not going to St. Petersburg, and that we were not particularly eager to pay out fifty-five marks for the mere fun of spending money. If the choice were left to us we felt that we could invest it more to our satisfaction in belts and card-cases.

He was very big and handsome, this German, and doubtless

some meek *fraeulein* loves him, but we do not, and, moreover, we pity her, whoever and wherever she may be, for we know by experience that if they two are ever to be made one he will be that one. He said he was sorry, but that, doubtless, when we got to the Russian frontier we could explain matters and get our trunks. But we could not speak Russian, we told him, and we wanted things properly arranged then and there. He clicked his heels together and bowed in a superb manner, and we were sure our eloquence and our distress had fetched him, so to speak, when to our amazement he simply reiterated his statements.

"But surely you are not going to let two American women leave your hotel all alone at eleven o'clock at night with their luggage checked to the wrong town?" I said, in wide-eyed astonishment.

Again he clicked those heels of his. Again that silk hat came off. Again that superb bow. He was very sorry, but he could do nothing. Doubtless we could arrange things at the frontier. It was within ten minutes of train time, and we were surrounded by no fewer than thirty German men—guests, porters, hall-boys—who listened curiously, and offered no assistance.

I looked at my companion, and she looked at me, and ground her teeth.

"Then you absolutely refuse us the courtesy of walking across the street with us and mending matters, do you?" I said.

Again those heels, that hat, that bow. I could have killed him. I am sorry now that I didn't. I missed a glorious opportunity.

So off we started alone at eleven o'clock at night for Poland, with our trunks safely checked through to St. Petersburg, and fifty-five marks lighter in pocket.

My companion kept saying, "Well, I never!" A pause. And again, "Well, I never!" And again, "Did you ever in all your life!" Yet there was no sameness in my ears to her remarks, for it was all that I, too, wanted to say. It covered the ground completely.

I was speechless with surprise. It kept recurring to my mind that my friends in America who had lived in Germany had told me that I need expect nothing at the hands of German men on account of being a woman. I couldn't seem to get it through my head. But now that it had happened to me—now that a man had deliberately refused to cross the street—no farther, mind you!—to get us out of such a mess! Why, in America, there isn't a man from the President to a chimney-sweep, from a major-general to the blackest nigger in the cotton fields, who wouldn't do ten times that much for *any* woman!

I shall never get over it.

With the courage of despair I accosted every man and woman on the platform with the words, "Do you speak English?" But not one of them did. Nor French either. So with heavy hearts we got on the train, feed the porter four marks for getting us into this dilemma (and incidentally carrying our hand-luggage), and when he had the impertinence to demand more I turned on him and assured him that if he dared to speak another word to us we would report him to His Excellency the American Ambassador, who was on intimate terms with the Kaiser; and that I would use my influence to have him put in prison for life. He fled in dismay, although I know he did not understand one word.

My manner, however, was not affable. Then I cast myself into my berth in a despairing heap, and broke two of the wings in my hat.

My companion was almost in tears. "Never mind," she said. "It was all my fault. But we may get our trunks, anyway. And if not, perhaps we can get along without them."

"Impossible!" I said. "How can we spend a week as guests in a house without a change of clothes?"

In order not to let her know how worried I was, I told her that if we couldn't get our trunks off the train at Vilna we would give up our visit and telegraph our excuses and regrets to our expectant hostess, or else come back from St. Petersburg after we had got our precious trunks once more within our clutches.

All the next day we tried to find some one who spoke English or French, but to no avail. We spent, therefore, a dreary day. By letting my companion manage the customs officers in patomime we got through the frontier without having to unlock anything, although it is considered the most difficult one in Europe.

The trains in Russia fairly crawl. Instead of coal they use wood in their engines, which sends back thousands of sparks like the tail of a comet. It grew dark about two o'clock in the afternoon, and we found ourselves promenading through the bleakest of winter landscapes. Tiny cottages, emitting a bright red glow from infinitesimal windows, crouched in the snow, and silent fir-trees silhouetted themselves against the moonlit sky. It only needed the howl of wolves to make it the loneliest picture the mind could conceive.

When we were within an hour of Vilna I heard in the

distance my companion's familiar words, "Pardon me, sir, but do you speak English?" And a deep voice, which I knew without seeing him came from a big man, replied in French, "For the first time in my life I regret that I do not."

At the sound of French I hurried to the door of our compartment, and there stood a tall Russian officer in his gray uniform and a huge fur-lined pelisse which came to his feet.

When my companion wishes to be amusing she says that as soon as I found that the man spoke French I whirled her around by the arm and sent her spinning into the corner among the valises. But I don't remember even touching her. I only remembered that here was some one to whom I could talk, and in two minutes this handsome Russian had untangled my incoherent explanations, had taken our luggage receipt, and had assured us that he himself would not pause until he had seen our trunks taken from the train at Vilna. If I should live a thousand years I never shall forget nor cease to be grateful to that superb Russian. He was so very much like an American gentleman.

We were met at the station by our Polish friends, our precious trunks were put into sledges, we were stowed into the most comfortable of equipages, and in an hour we were installed in one of the most delightful homes it was ever my good fortune to enter.

I never realized before what people can suffer at the hands of a conquering government, and were it not that the young Tzar of Russia has done away, either by public ukase or private advice, with the worst of the wrongs his father permitted to be put upon the Poles, I could not bear to listen to their recitals.

Politics, as a rule, make little impression upon me. Guide-books are a bore, and histories are unattractive, they are so dry and accurate. My father's grief at my lack of essential knowledge is perennial and deep-seated. But, somehow, facts are the most elusive things I have to contend with. I can only seem to get a firm grasp on the imaginary. Of course, I know the historical facts in this case, but it does not sound personally pathetic to read that Russia, Prussia, and Austria divided Poland between them.

But to be here in Russia, in what was once Poland, visiting the families of the Polish nobility; to see their beautiful home-life, their marvellous family affection, the respect they pay to their women; to feel all the charm of their broad culture and noble sympathy for all that makes for the general good, and then to hear the story of their oppression, is to feel a personal ache in the heart for their national burdens.

It does not sound as if a grievous hardship were being put upon a conquered people to read in histories or guide-books that Prussia is colonizing her part of Poland with Germans—selling them land for almost nothing in order to infuse German blood, German language, German customs into a conquered land. It does not touch one's sympathies very much to know that Austria is the only one of the three to give Poland the most of her rights, and in a measure to restore her self-respect by allowing her representation in the Reichstag and by permitting Poles to hold office.

But when you come to Russian Poland and know that in the province of Lithuania—which was a separate and distinct province until a prince of Lithuania fell in love with and married a queen of Poland, and the two countries were joined—Poles are not allowed to buy one foot of land in the country where they were born and bred, are not permitted to hold office even when elected, are prohibited from speaking their own language in public, are forbidden to sing their Polish hymns, or to take children in from the streets and teach them in anything but Russian, and that every one is taught the Greek religion, then this colonization becomes a burning question. Then you know how to appreciate America, where we have full, free, and unqualified liberty.

The young Tzar has greatly endeared himself to his Polish subjects by several humane and generous acts. One was to remove the tax on all estates (over and above the ordinary taxes), which Poles were obliged to pay annually to the Russian government. Another was to release school-children from the necessity of attending the Greek church on all Russian feast-days. These two were by public ukase, and as the Poles are passionately grateful for any act of kindness, one hears nothing but good words for the Tzar, and there is the utmost feeling of loyalty to him among them. I hear it constantly said that if he continue in this generous policy Russia need never apprehend another Polish revolution. And while by a revolution they could never hope to accomplish anything, there being now but fourteen million Poles to contend against these three powerful nations, still, as long as they have one about every thirty-five years, perhaps it is a wise precaution on the part of the young Tzar to begin with his kindness promptly, as it is about time for another one!

Another recent thing which the Poles attribute to the Tzar was the removal from the street corners, the shops, the railroad stations, and the clubs, of the placards forbidding the Polish language to be spoken in public.

Thus the Poles hope much from the young Tzar in the future, and believe that he would do more were he not held back by Russian public opinion. For example, the other day two Russians were overheard in the train to say: "For thirty years we have tried to force our religion on the Poles, our language on the Poles, and our customs on the Poles, but now here comes 'The Little Colonel' (the young Tzar), and in a moment he sweeps away all the progress we had made."

To call him "The Little Colonel" is a term of great endearment, and the name arose from the fact that by some strange oversight he was never made a General by his father, but remained at the death of the late Tzar only a Colonel. When urged by his councillors to make himself General, as became a Tzar of all the Russias, he said: "No. The power which should have made me a General is no more. Now that I am at the head of the government I surely could not be so conceited as to promote myself."

The misery among the poor in Poland is almost beyond belief, yet all charities for them must be conducted secretly, for the government stills forbids the establishment of kindergartens or free schools where Polish children would be taught in the Polish language. I have been questioned very closely about our charities in America, especially in Chicago, and I have given them all the working plans of the college settlements, the kindergartens, and the sewing-schools. The Poles are a wonderfully sympathetic and warm-hearted people, and are anxious to ameliorate the bitter poverty which exists here to an enormous extent. They sigh in vain for the freedom with which we may proceed, and regard Americans as seated in the very lap of a luxurious government because we are at liberty to give our money to any cause without being interfered with.

One of the noblest young women I have ever met is a Polish countess, wealthy, beautiful, and fascinating, who has turned her back upon society and upon the brilliant marriage her family had hoped for her, and has taken a friend who was at the head of a London training-school for nurses to live with her upon her estates, and these two have consecrated their lives to the service of the poor. They will educate Polish nurses to use in private charity. With no garb, no creed, no blare of trumpet, they have made themselves into "Little Sisters of the Poor."

I could not fail to notice the difference in the young girls as soon as I crossed the Russian frontier and came into the land of the Slav. Here at once I found individuality. Polish girls are more like American girls. If you ask a young English girl what she thinks of Victor Hugo she tells you that her mamma does not allow her to read French novels. If you ask a French girl how she likes to live in Paris she tells you that she never went down town alone in her life.

But the Polish girls are different. They are individual. They all have a personality. When you have met one you never feel as if you had met all. In this respect they resemble American girls, but only in this respect, for whereas there is a type of Polish young girl—and a charming type she is—I never in my life saw what I considered a really typical American girl. You cannot typify the psychic charm of the young American girl. It is altogether beyond you.

These Polish girls who have titles are as simple and unaffected as possible. I had no difficulty in calling their mothers Countess and Princess, etc., but I tripped once or twice with the young girls, whereat they begged me in the sweetest way to call them by their first names without any prefix. They were charming. They taught us the Polish mazurka—a dance which has more go to it than any dance I ever saw. It requires the Auditorium ball-room to dance it in, and enough breath to play the trombone in an orchestra. The officers dance with their spurs on, which jingle and click in an exciting manner, and to my surprise never seem to catch in the women's gowns.

The home life of the Poles is very beautiful; and, in particular, the deference paid to the father and mother strikes my American sensibilities forcibly. I never tire of watching the entrance into the salon of the married sons of the Countess when each comes to pay his daily visit to his mother. They are all four tall, impressive, and almost majestic, with a curious hawk-like quality in their glance, which may be an inheritance from their warrior forefathers. Count Antoine comes in just before going home to dine, while we are all assembled and dressed for dinner. He flings the door open, and makes his military bow to the room, then making straight for his mother's chair, he kneels at her feet, kisses her hand and then her brow, and sometimes again her hand. Then he passes the others, and kisses his sister on the cheek, and after thus saluting all the members of his family, he turns to us, the guests, and speaks to us.

The Poles are the most individual and interesting people I have yet encountered. The men in particular are fascinating, and a man who is truly fascinating in the highest sense of the word; one whose character is worth study, and whose friendship would repay cultivating as sincerely as many of the Poles I know, is a boon to thank God for.

Before I came to Poland it always surprised me to realize that so many men and women of world-wide genius came from so small a nation. But now that I have had the opportunity of knowing them intimately and of studying their characteristics, both nationally and individually, I see why.

Poland is the home of genius by right. Her people, even if they never write or sing or act or play, have all the elements in their character which go to make up that complex commodity known as genius, whether it ever becomes articulate or not. You feel that they could all do things if they tried. They are a sympathetic, interesting, interested, and, above all, a magnetic people. This forms the top soil for a nation which has put forth so much of wonder and sweetness to enrich the world, but the reason which lies deep down at the root of the matter for the *soul* which thrills through all this melody of song and story is in the sorrowful and tragic history of this nation.

The Poles are a race of burning patriots. To-day they are as keen over national sufferings and national wrongs as on that unfortunate clay when they went into a fiercely unwilling and resentful captivity. Their pride, their courage, their bitterness of spirit, their longing for revenge now no longer find an outlet on the battlefield. Yet it smoulders continually in their innermost being. You must crush the heart, you must subdue a people, you must be no stranger to anguish and loss if you would discover the singer and the song. And so Poland's fierce and unrelenting patriotism has placed the divine spark of a genius which thrills a world in souls whose sweetest song is a cry wrung from a patriot's heart.

VI

ST. PETERSBURG

It behooves one to be good in Russia, for no matter how excellent your reputation at home, no matter how long you have been a member in good and regular standing of the most orthodox church, no matter how innocent your heart may be of anarchy, nihilism, or murder, you travel, you rest, you eat, sleep, wake, or dream, tracked by the Russian police.

They snatch your passport the moment you arrive at a hotel, and register you, and if you change your hotel every day, every day your passport is taken, and you are requested to fill out a blank with your name, age, religion, nationality, and the name and hotel of the town where you were last.

When we entered our Russian hotel—when we had entirely entered, I mean, for we passed through six or eight swinging doors with moujiks to open and shut each one, and bow and scrape at our feet—we found ourselves in a stiflingly hot corridor, where the odor was a combination of smoke and people whose furs needed airing.

It would be an excellent idea if Americans who live in cold climates dressed as sensibly as Russians do. They keep their houses about as warm as we keep ours, but they wear thin clothing indoors and put on their enormous furs for the street. On entering any house, church, shop, or theatre, the chuba and overshoes are removed, and although they spend half their lives putting them on and taking them off, yet the other half is comfortable.

The women seem to have no pride about the appearance of their feet, for now the doctors are ordering them to wear the common gray felt boot of the peasants, with the top of it reaching to the knee. It is without doubt the most hideous and unshapely object the mind can conceive, being all made of one piece and without any regard to the shape of the foot.

St. Petersburg can hardly be called a typical Russian city. It is too near other countries, but to us, before we had seen Moscow and Kiev, it was Russia itself. We arrived one bitterly cold day, and went first to the hotel to which we had been recommended by our friends.

I shall never forget the wave of longing for home and country which settled down upon me as we saw our rooms in this hotel. It must have been built in Peter the Great's time. No electric lights; not even lamps. Candles! Now, if there is one thing more than another which makes me frantic with homesickness, it is the use of candles. I would rather be in London on Sunday than to dress by the light of candles.

Even an excellent luncheon did not raise my spirits. Our rooms were as dark and gloomy and silent as a mausoleum. Indeed, many a mausoleum I have seen has been much more cheerful. It was at the time of year also when we had but three hours of daylight—from eleven until two. Our salon was furnished in a dreary drab, with a gigantic green stove in the corner which reached to the ceiling. Then we entered what looked like a long, narrow corridor, down which we blindly felt our way, and at the extreme end of which were hung dark red plush curtains, as if before a shrine. We pulled aside these trappings of gloom, and there were two iron cots, not over a foot and a half wide, about the shape and feeling of an ironing-board, covered with what appeared to be gray army blankets, I looked to see "U.S." stamped on them. I have seen them in museums at home.

I gazed at my companion in perfect dismay. "I shall not present a single letter of introduction," I wailed. "I'm going to Moscow to-morrow."

Instead of going to Moscow in the morning, we went out and decided to present just the one letter to our ambassador. He was at the Hotel d'Europe, and we went there. Behold! electric lights everywhere. Heaps of Americans. And the entire Legation there. My companion and I simply looked at each other, and our whole future grew brighter. We would not go to Moscow, but we would move at once. We would introduce electricity into our sombre lives, and look forward with hope into the great unknown. We rushed around and presented all the rest of our letters, and went back to spend a wretched evening with eight candles and a smoky lamp.

The next day we called for our bill and prepared to move. To my disgust, I found an item of two rubles for the use of that lamp. I had serious thoughts of opening up communication with the Standard Oil Company by cable. But we were so delighted with our new accommodations in prospect that we left the hotel in a state of exhilaration that nothing could dampen.

To our great disappointment we found a number of Americans leaving St. Petersburg for Moscow because the Hermitage was closed. Now, the Hermitage and the ceremony of the Blessing of the Waters of the Neva were what I most wished to see, but we were informed at the Legation that we could have neither wish gratified. However, my spirit was undaunted. It was only the American officials who had pronounced it impossible. My lucky star had gone with me so far, and had opened so many unaccustomed doors, that I did not despair. I said I would see what our letters of introduction brought forth.

We did not have to wait long. No sooner had we presented our letters than people came to see us, and placed themselves at our disposal for days and even weeks at a time. Their kindness and hospitality were too charming for mere words to express.

Although the Winter Palace was closed to visitors, preparatory to the arrival on the next day of the Tzar and Tzarina, it was opened for us through the influence of the daughter of the Commodore of the late Tzar's private yacht, Mademoiselle de Falk, who took us through it. It was simply superb, and was, of course, in perfect readiness for the arrival of the imperial family, with all the gorgeous crimson velvet carpets spread, and the plants and flowers arranged in the Winter Garden.

Then, through this same influential friend, the Hermitage— the second finest and the very richest museum in all Europe—was opened for us, and—well, I kept my head going through the show palaces in London, and Paris, and Berlin, and Dresden, and Potsdam, but I lost it completely in the Hermitage. Then and there I absolutely went crazy. A whole guide-book devoted simply to the Hermitage could give no sort of idea of the barbaric splendor of its belongings. Its riches are beyond belief. Even the presents given by the Emir of Bokhara to the Tzar are splendid enough to dazzle one like a realization of the Arabian Nights. But to see the most valuable of all, which are kept in the

Emperor's private vaults, is to be reduced to a state of bewilderment bordering on idiocy.

It is astonishing enough, to one who has bought even one Russian belt set with turquoise enamel, to think of all the trappings of a horse—bit, bridle, saddle-girth, saddlecloth, and all, made of cloth of gold and set in solid turquoise enamel; with the sword hilt, scabbard, belts, pistol handle and holster made of the same. Well, these are there by the dozen. Then you come to the private jewels, and you see all these same accoutrements made of precious stones—one of solid diamonds; another of diamonds, emeralds, topazes, and rubies. And the size of these stones! Why, you never would believe me if I should tell you how large they are. Many of them are uncut and badly set, from an English stand-point. But in quantity and size—well, I was glad to get back to my three-ruble-a-day room and to look at my one trunk, and to realize that my own humble life would go on just the same, and my letter of credit would not last any longer for all the splendors which exist for the Tzar of all the Russias.

The churches in St. Petersburg are so magnificent that they, too, go to your head. We did nothing but go to mass on Christmas Eve and Christmas Day, for although we spent our Christmas in Berlin, we arrived in St. Petersburg in time for the Russian Christmas, which comes twelve days later than ours. St. Isaac's, the Kazan, and Sts. Peter and Paul dazed me. The icons or images of the Virgin are set with diamonds and emeralds worth a king's ransom. They are only under glass, which is kept murky from the kisses which the people press upon the hands and feet.

The interiors of the cathedrals, with their hundreds of silver *couronnes*, and battle-flags, and trophies of conquests, look like great bazaars. Every column is covered clear to the dome. The tombs of the Tzars are always surrounded by people, and candles burn the year round. Upon the tomb of Alexander II., under glass, is the exquisite laurel wreath placed there by President Faure. It is of gold, and was made by Falize, one of the most famous carvers of gold in Europe.

The famous mass held on Christmas Eve in the cathedral of St. Isaac was one of the most beautiful services I ever attended. In the first place, St. Isaac's is the richest church in all Russia. It has, too, the most wonderful choir, for the Tzar loves music, and wherever in all his Empire a beautiful voice is found, the boy is brought to St. Petersburg and educated by the State to enter the Emperor's choir. When we entered the church the service had been in progress for five hours. That immense church was packed to suffocation. In the Greek church every one stands, no matter how long the service. In fact, you cannot sit down unless you sit on the floor, for there are no seats.

By degrees we worked our way towards the space reserved for the Diplomatic Corps, where we were invited to enter. Our wraps were taken and chairs were given to us. We found ourselves on the platform with the priest, just back of the choir. What heavenly voices! What wonderful voices! The bass holds on to the last note, and the rumble and echo of it rolls through those vaulted domes like the tones of an organ. The long-haired priest, too, had a wonderful resonant voice for intoning. He passed directly by us in his gorgeous cloth of gold vestments, as he went out.

The instant he had finished, the little choir boys began to pinch each other and thrust their tapers in each other's faces, and behaved quite like ordinary boys. The great crowd scattered and huge ladders were brought in to put out the hundreds of candles in the enormous chandeliers. Religion was over, and the world began again.

The other art which is maintained at the government expense is the ballet. We went several times, and it was very gorgeous. It is all pantomime—not a word is spoken—but so well done that one does not tire of it.

Every one sympathized so with us because we could not see the ceremony of the Blessing of the Waters of the Neva, and our ambassador apologized for not being able to arrange it, and we said, "Not at all," and "Pray, do not mention it," at the same time secretly hoping that our Russian friends, who were putting forth strenuous efforts on our behalf, would be able to manage it.

On the morning of the 18th of January a note came from a Russian officer who was on duty at the Winter Palace, saying that Baron Elsner, the Secretary of the Prefect of Police, would call for us with his carriage at ten o'clock, and we would be conducted to the private space reserved just in front of the Winter Palace, where the best view of everything could be obtained. My companion and I fell into each other's arms in wild delight, for it had been most difficult to manage, and we had not been sure until that very moment.

Now, the person of the Tzar is so sacred that it is forbidden by law even to represent him on the stage, and as to photographing him—a Russian faints at the mere thought. Nevertheless, we wished very much to photograph this pageant, so we determined, if possible, to take our camera. Everything else that we wanted had been done for us ever since we started, and our faith was strong that we would get this. At first the stout heart of Baron Elsner quailed at our suggestion. Then he said to take the camera with us, which we did with joy. His card parted the crowd right and left, and our carriage drove through long lines of soldiers, and between throngs of people held in check by mounted police, and by rows of infantry, who locked arms and made of themselves a living wall, against which the crowd surged.

To our delight we found our places were not twenty feet from the entrance to the Winter Palace. We noticed Baron Elsner speaking to several officials, and we heard the word "Americanski," which had so often opened hearts and doors to us, for Russia honestly likes America, and presently the Baron said, in a low tone, "When the Emperor passes out you may step down here; these soldiers will surround you, and you may photograph him."

I could scarcely believe my ears. I was so excited that I nearly dropped the camera.

The procession moves only about one hundred feet—a crimson carpet being laid from the entrance of the Winter Palace, across the street, and up into a pavilion which is built out over the Neva.

First came the metropolitans and the priests; then the Emperor's celebrated choir of about fifty voices; then a detachment of picked officers bearing the most important battle-flags from the time of Peter the Great, which showed the marks of sharp conflict; then the Emperor's suite, and then—the Emperor himself. They all marched with bared heads, even the soldiers.

My companion had the opera-glasses, I had the camera. "Tell me when," I gasped. They passed before me in a sort of haze. I heard the band in the Winter Palace and the singing of the choir. I heard the splash of the cross which the Archbishop plunged into the opening that had been cut in the ice. I heard the priests intone, and the booming of the guns firing the imperial salute. I saw that the wind was blowing the candles out. Then came a breathless pause, and then she said,

"Now!" A little click. It was done; I had photographed Nicholas II., the Tzar of all the Russias!

VII

RUSSIA

Yesterday we had our first Russian experience in the shape of a troika ride. Russians, as a rule, do not troika except at night. In fact, from my experience, they reverse the established order of things and turn night into day.

A troika is a superb affair. It makes the tiny sledges which take the place of cabs, and are used for all ordinary purposes, look even more like toys than usual. But the sledges are great fun, and so cheap that it is an extravagance to walk. A course costs only twenty kopecks—ten cents. The sledges are set so low that you can reach out and touch the snow with your hand, and they are so small that the horse is in your lap and the coachman in your pocket. He simply turns in his seat to hook the fur robe to the back of your seat—only it has no back. If you fall, you fall clear to the ground.

The horse is far, far above you in your humble position, and there is so little room that two people can with difficulty stow themselves in the narrow seat. If a brother and sister or a husband and wife drive together, the man, in sheer self-defence, is obliged to put his arm around the woman, no matter how distasteful it may be. Not that she would ever be conscious of whether he did it or not, for the amount of clothes one is obliged to wear in Russia destroys any sense of touch.

The idvosjik, or coachman, is so bulky from this same reason that you cannot see over him. You are obliged to crane your neck to one side. His head is covered with a Tartar cap. He wears his hair down to his collar, and then chopped off in a straight line. His pelisse is of a bluish gray, fits tightly to the waist, and comes to the feet. But the skirt of it is gathered on back and front, giving him an irresistibly comical pannier effect, like a Dolly Varden polonaise. The Russian idvosjik guides his horse curiously. He coaxes it forward by calling it all sorts of pet names—"doushka," darling, etc. Then he beats it with a toy whip, which must feel like a fly on its woolly coat, for all the little fat pony does is to kick up its heels and fly along like the wind, missing the other sledges by a hair's-breadth. It is ghostly to see the way they glide along without a sound, for the sledges wear no bells.

One may drive with perfect safety at a breakneck pace, for they all drive down on one side of the street and up on the other. Nor will an idvosjik hesitate to use his whip about the head and face of another idvosjik who dares to turn without crossing the street.

He stops his horse with a guttural trill, as if one should say "Tr-r-r-r-r" in the back of the throat. It sounds like a gargle.

The horses are sharp-shod, but in a way quite different from ours. The spikes on their shoes are an inch long, and dig into the ice with perfect security, but it makes the horses look as if they wore French heels. Even over ice like sheer glass they go at a gallop and never slip. It is wonderful, and the exhilaration of it is like driving through an air charged with champagne, like the wine-caves of Rintz.

Our troika was like a chariot in comparison with these sledges. It was gorgeously upholstered in red velvet, and held six—three on each seat. The robes also were red velvet, bordered and lined with black bear fur. There were three horses driven abreast. The middle horse was much larger than the other two, and wore a high white wooden collar, which stood up from the rest of the harness, and was hung with bells and painted with red flowers and birds.

To my delight the horses were wild, and stood on their hind legs and bit each other, and backed us off the road, and otherwise acted like Tartar horses in books. It seemed almost too good to be true. It was like driving through the Black Forest and seeing the gnomes and the fairies one has read about. I told my friends very humbly that I had never done anything in my life to deserve the good fortune of having those beautiful horses act in such a satisfactory and historical manner. We had to get out twice and let the idvosjik calm them down. But even when ploughing my way out of snow up to my knees I breathed an ecstatic sigh of gratitude and joy. I could not understand the men's annoyance. It was too ideal to complain about.

We drove out to the Island for luncheon, and on the way we stopped and coasted in a curious Russian sledge from the top of a high place, something like our toboggan-slides, only this sledge was guided from behind by a peasant on skates.

A Russian meal always begins with a side-table of *hors d'oeuvres*, called "zakouska." That may not be spelled right, but no Russian would correct me, because the language is phonetic, and they spell the same word in many different ways. Their alphabet has thirty-eight letters in it, besides the little marks to tell you whether to make a letter hard or soft.

Even proper names take on curious oddities of spelling, and

a husband and wife or two brothers will spell their name differently when using the Latin letters. If you complain about it, and ask which is correct, they make that famous Russian reply which Bismarck once had engraved in his ring, and which he believed brought him such good luck, "Neechy voe," "It is nothing," or "Never mind." You can spell with your eyes shut in Russian, and you simply cannot make a mistake, for the Russians spell with all the abandonment of French dancing.

This zakouska is so delicious and so varied and so tempting that one not accustomed to it eats too much without realizing. At a dinner an American looked at my loaded plate and said, with delicious impertinence, "Confidentially, I don't mind telling you that dinner is *coming*."

As we came back, the full delight of troika-riding came over us, for driving in the country we could not tell how fast we were going. But in town, whizzing past other carriages, hearing the shouts of the idvosjik, "Troika!" and seeing the people scatter and the sledges turn out (for a troika has the right of way), we realized at what a pace we were going. We dashed across the frozen Neva, with its tramway built right on the ice; past the Winter Palace, along the quai, where all the embassies are, into the Grand Morskaia, and from there into the Nevski, with the snow flying and our bells ringing, and the middle horse trotting and the outer horses galloping, sending clouds of steam from their heaving flanks and palpitating nostrils, and the biting air making our blood tingle, and the reiterated shout of the idvosjik, "Troika! troika!" taking our breath away.

We had one more excitement before we reached home, which was seeing a Russian fire-engine. We passed it in a run. The engine was on one sledge, and following it were five other sledges carrying hogsheads of water.

I am glad we came to Russia in winter, for by so doing we have met the Russian people, the most fascinating that any country can boast, with the charm of the French, the courage of the English, the sentiment of the Germans, the sincerity and hospitality of the Americans. Their courtesy to each other is a never-ending pleasure to me. Poles and Russians treat their women more nearly the way our American men treat us than any nation we have encountered so far. They are the most marvellous linguists in the world. We have met no one in Russia who speaks fewer than three languages, and we have met several who speak twelve. They are not arrogant even concerning their military strength. They are quite modest about their learning and their not inconsiderable literary and artistic achievements, and they hold themselves, both nationally and individually, in the plastic state where they are willing to learn from any nation or any master who can teach what they wish to know. There is a marvellous future for Russia, for their riches and resources are as vast and inestimable as their possessions. They themselves do not realize how mighty they are.

Here is France grovelling at their feet, spending millions of francs to entertain the Tzar—France, a nation which must see a prospect of double her money returned before she parts with a sou; with the cathedrals filled with *couronnes* sent by the French press; with no compliment to Russia too fulsome for French gallantry to invent finding space in the foremost French newspapers; hoping, praying, beseeching the help of Russia, when Germany makes up her mind to gobble France, yet dealing Russian achievement a backhanded slap by hinting what a compliment it is for a cultivated, accomplished, over-cultured race like the French to beg the assistance of a barbarous country like Russia.

I believe that Russia is the only country in the world which feels nationally friendly and individually interested in

America. I used to think France was, and I held Lafayette firmly and proudly in my memory to prove it. But I was promptly undeceived as to their individual interest, and when I still clung to Lafayette as a proof of the former I was laughed to scorn and told that France as a nation had nothing to do with that; that Lafayette went to America as a soldier of fortune. He would just as soon have gone to Madagascar or Timbuctoo, but America was accommodating enough to have a war on just in time to serve his ambition. If that is true, I wish they had not told me. I would like to come home with a few ideals left—if they will permit me.

When I was in Berlin I asked our ambassador, Mr. White, what Germany thought of America. He replied, "Just what Thackeray thought of Tupper. When some one asked Thackeray what he thought of Tupper, he replied, 'I don't think of him at all.'"

But in Russia I have a sore throat all the time from answering questions about America. I think I am not exaggerating when I say I have answered a million in a single evening. My companion at first was disgusted with my wearing myself out in such a manner, but I said, "I am so grateful to them for *caring*, after the indifference of all these other self-sufficient countries, that I am willing to sacrifice myself at it if necessary."

We never realized how little we knew about America until we discovered the Russian capacity for asking unexpected questions. I bought an American history in Russia, and sat up nights trying to remember what my father had tried to instil into my sieve-like brain. After a week of witnessing my feverish enthusiasm, even my companion's dormant national pride was roused. She, too, was ashamed to say, "I don't know," when they asked us these terrible questions. When we get into the clutches of a party of women we trust to luck that they cannot remember our statistics long enough to tell their husbands and brothers (I have a horror of men's accuracy in figures), and we calmly guess at the answers when our exact knowledge gives out.

One night they attacked my companion on the school question. Now, she does not know one solitary thing about the public-school system, but, to my utter amazement, I heard her giving the number of children between the ages of eight and ten who were in the public schools in the State of Illinois, and then running them off by counties. I was afraid she would soon begin to call the roll of their names from memory, so I rescued her and took her home. I suppose we must have an air of intelligence which successfully masks our colossal ignorance of occult facts and defunct dates, because they rely on us to inform them off-hand concerning everything social, political, historical, sacred and profane, spirituous and spiritual, from the protoplasm of the cliff-dwellers to the details of the Dingley bill, not skipping accurate information on the process of whiskey-making in Kentucky, a crocodile-hunt in Florida, suffrage in Wyoming, a lynching-bee in Texas, polygamy in Utah, prune-drying in California, divorces in Dakota, gold-mining in Colorado, cotton-spinning in Georgia, tobacco-raising in Alabama, marble-quarrying in Tennessee, the number of Quakers in Philadelphia, one's sensations while being scalped by Sioux, how marriages are arranged, what a man says when he proposes, the details of a camp-meeting, a description of a negro baptism, and the main arguments on the silver question.

They get some curious ideas in their heads concerning us, but they are so amazingly well informed about America that their specific misinformation never irritated me. The small use they have for their English sometimes accounts for the queer things they say.

The official costume for men who have no particular uniform is regulation evening dress, which they are obliged to wear all day. They become so tired of it that this is the reason, they tell me, why so many men, even in smart society, go to the opera or even dinners in frock-coats. One one occasion a most intelligent man said to me, "I am told that in America the ladies always wear decollete costumes at dinners, and the men are always in night-dress."

For one hysterical moment my mind's eye pictured a dinner-table on Prairie Avenue with alternately a low-necked gown and a pair of pajamas, and I choked. Then I happened to think that he meant "evening dress," and I recovered sufficiently to explain.

The Tzarina has made English the Court language, and since her coronation no state balls take place on Sunday.

Russian hospitality is delightful. We could remain a year in Russia and not exhaust our invitations to visit at their country-houses. Russia must be beautiful in summer, but if you wish to go into society, to know the best of the people, to see their sweet home life, and to understand how they live and enjoy themselves, you must go in the winter. I cannot think what any one would find of national life in summer in Russia, for everybody has a country-house and everybody goes to it and leaves the city to tourists.

Russia, in spite of her vast riches, has not arrived at supercivilization, where there is corruption in the very atmosphere. She is an undeveloped and a young country, and while the Tzar is wise and kind and beneficent, and an excellent Tzar as Tzars go, still Russians, even the best and most enlightened of them, are slaves. I have met a number of the gentlest and cleverest men who had been exiled to Siberia, and pardoned. Their picture-galleries bear witness to this underlying sadness of knowing that in spite of everything they are not *free*. All their actions are watched, their every word listened to, spies are everywhere, the police are omnipresent, and over all their gayety and vivacity and mirth and spontaneity there is the constant fear of the awful hand in whose complete power they are. His clemency, his fatherhood to his people, his tremendous responsibility for their welfare are all appreciated, but the thought is in every mind, "When will this kindness fail? Upon whose head will the lightning descend next?"

Title and gentle birth and the long and faithful service of one's ancestors to the Tzars are of small avail if the evidence should go against one in Russia. I have heard princes say less than I have said here, but say it in whispers and with furtive looks at the nearest man or woman. I have seen their starts of surprise at the frank impudence of our daring to criticise our administration in their midst, and I felt as if I were in danger of being bombarded from the back.

In Russia you may spell as you please, but you must have a care how you criticise the government. In America you may criticise the government as you will, but you must have a care how you spell.

VIII

MOSCOW

I thought St. Petersburg interesting, but it is modern compared to Moscow. Everything is so strange and curious here. The churches, the chimes, the palace, the coronation chapel, and the street scenes are enough to drive one mad with interest.

Moscow is said to have sixteen hundred churches, and I really think we did not skip one. They are almost as magnificent as those in St. Petersburg, and they impressed— overpowered us, in fact, with the same unspeakable riches of the Greek Church.

The name of our hotel was so curious that I cannot forbear repeating it, "The Slavansky Bazaar," and they call their smartest restaurant "The Hermitage." I felt as if I could be sold at auction in "The Bazaar," and as if I ought to fast and pray in "The Hermitage."

"The Slavansky Bazaar" was one of the dirtiest hotels it ever was my lot to see. The Russians of the middle class—to say nothing of the peasants, who are simply unspeakable—are not a clean set, so one cannot blame a hotel for not living above the demands of its *clientele*. There were some antique specimens of cobwebs in our rooms, which made restful corner ornaments with dignified festoons, which swung slowly to and fro with such fascinating solemnity that I could not leave off looking at them. The hotel is built up hill and down dale, and each corridor smells more musty than the other. It has a curious arrangement for supplying water in the rooms which I never can recall with any degree of pleasure. One evening after I had dressed I went to the wash-stand and discovered that there was no water. I was madly ringing for the chambermaid when my companion called from her room, and said, "Put your foot on that brass thing. There is plenty of water."

I looked down, and near the floor was a brass pedal, like that of a piano. Sure enough, there was a reservoir above and a faucet with the head of a dragon on it peering up into my face, which I never had noticed before. Now, the pedal of my piano works hard, so I bent all my strength to this one, and lo! from that impudent dragon's mouth I got a mighty stream of water straight in my unconscious face, and enough to put out a fire. I fell back with a shriek of astonishment and indignation, and my companion laughed—nay, she roared. She laughs until she cries even now every time she thinks of it, although I had to change my gown. How was *I* going to know that I was leaning over a waterspout, I should like to know!

In this same hotel when I asked for a blotter they brought me a box of sand. I tried to use it, but my hand was not very steady, and none of it went on the letter. Some got in my shoe, however.

But our environments were more than compensated for by the exceeding kindness that we received from the most delightful people that it ever was my good fortune to meet, and their attentions to us were so charming that we shall remember them as long as we live.

Americans, even though we are as hospitable as any nation on earth, might well take a lesson from the Russians in regard to the respect they pay to a letter of introduction. The English send word when you can be received, and you pay each other frosty formal calls, and then are asked to five-o'clock tea or some other wildly exciting function of similar importance. The French are great sticklers for etiquette, but they are more spontaneous, and you are asked to dine at once. After that it is your own fault if you are not asked again. But in Russia it is different. I think that the men must have accompanied my messenger home, and the women to whom I presented letters early in the afternoon were actually waiting for me when I returned from presenting the last ones. In Moscow they came and waited hours for my return. I was mortified that there were not four of me to respond to all the beauties of their friendship, for hospitality in Russia includes even that.

They placed themselves, their carriages, their servants, at our disposal for whatever we had to do—sight-seeing, shopping, or idling. Mademoiselle Yermoloff, lady-in-waiting to the two empresses, simply took us upon her hands to show us Russian society life. She came with her sledge in the morning, and kept us with her all day long, taking us to see the most interesting people and places in Moscow. She showed us the coronation-robes, the embroideries upon which were from her own beautiful designs. The Empress presented her with an emerald and diamond brooch in recognition of this important service, for undoubtedly the coronation-robe of the present Tzarina is much handsomer and in better taste than any of the others. The designs are so artistically sketched that they all have a special significance.

Here we visited the charming Princess Golitzine, a most

beautiful and accomplished woman. Her house, we were told, De Lesseps, the father of the Suez De Lesseps, used as his headquarters during the French occupation of Moscow.

Mademoiselle Yermoloff's sledge was a very beautiful one, but it was quite as low-set as all the others, and her footman stood behind. As there was no back to the seat of her sledge, and her horses were rather fiery and unmanageable, every time they halted without warning this solemn flunky pitched forward into our backs, a performance which would have upset the dignity of an English footman, but which did not seem to disturb him in the least.

Mademoiselle Yermoloff took us to see Madame Chabelskoi, whose contributions to the World's Fair were of so much value. I never saw a private collection of anything so rich, so varied, and of such historical value as her collection of all the provincial costumes of the peasants of Finland and Big and Little Russia. In addition to these she has the fete-day toilets as well. The Kokoshniks are all embroidered in seed-pearls and gold ornaments, and if she were not a fabulously rich woman she could never have got all these, for each one is authentic and has actually been worn. They are not copies.

But Moscow seems to take a peculiar national pride in preserving the historical monuments of her country. There is a museum there, with a complete set of all these costumes on wax figures, and they range all the way from the grotesque to the lovely.

Madame Chabelskoi is now doing a very pretty as well as a valuable and historical work. She has two accomplished daughters, and these young girls spend all their time in selecting peasant women with typical features, dressing them in these costumes, photographing them, and then coloring these photographs in water-colors. They are making ten copies of each, to make ten magnificent albums, which are to be presented to the ten greatest museums in the world. The Hermitage in St. Petersburg is to have one, the British Museum another, and so on. Only one was to go to America, and to my metropolitan dismay I found that it was *not* to go to Chicago. I shall not say where it was intended to go; I shall only say that with characteristic modesty I asked, in my most timid voice, why she did not present it to a museum in the city which she had already benefited so royally with her generosity, and which already held her name in affectionate veneration. It seemed to strike her for the first time that Chicago *was* the proper city in which to place that album, so she promised it to us! I thanked her with sincere gratitude, and retired from the field with a modest flush of victory on my brow. I cannot forbear a wicked chuckle, however, when I think of that other museum!

We dined many times at "The Hermitage," which is one of the smartest restaurants in Europe. The costumes of the waiters were too extraordinary not to deserve a passing mention. They consisted of a white cotton garment belted at the waist, with no collar, and a pair of flapping white trousers. They are always scrupulously clean—which is a wonder for Russian peasants—for they are made to change their clothes twice a day. They have a magnificent orchestrion instead of an orchestra here, and I could scarcely eat those beautiful dinners for listening to the music. We became so well acquainted with the repertoire that our friends, knowing our taste, ordered the music to match the courses. So instead of sherry with the soup, they ordered the intermezzo from "Cavalleria Rusticana." With the fish we had the overture to "William Tell." With the *entrecote* we had a pot-pourri from "Faust." With the fowl we had "Demon and Tamar," the Russian opera. With the rest we began on Wagner and worked up to that thrilling

"Tannhaeuser" overture, until I was ready to go home a nervous wreck from German music, as I always am.

A very interesting incident occurred while we were in Moscow. The Tzar decorated a non-commissioned officer for an act of bravery which well deserved it. He was in charge of the powder-magazines just outside of Moscow, and from the view I had of them I should say that the gunpowder is stored in pits in the ground.

Something caught fire right on top of one of these pits, and this young officer saw it. He had no time to send for water, and if he delayed, at any moment the whole magazine might explode; one pit would communicate with another, and perhaps the whole city would be endangered; so without a second's hesitation he and his men sprang into the fire and literally trod it out with their feet, running the risk of an explosion by concussion, as well as by a spark of fire. It was a superb act of courage, and the Tzar decorated this young sergeant with the order of Vladimir—one of the rarest decorations in all Russia. I am told that not over six living men possess it to-day. It was a beautiful thing for the Tzar thus to recognize this heroic deed.

When we left Moscow we were having our first real taste of Russian winter, for, strange to say, although so much farther south, the climate is much more severe than that of St. Petersburg.

My companion complained bitterly that we were not seeing anything of Russia because we came down from St. Petersburg at night, so we abandoned the courier train, and took the slow day-train for Kiev, the old capital of Russia, that she might see more of the country.

But now I come to my reward and her chagrin. Between

Moscow and Kiev we were snowed in for sixteen hours. It was between stations, the food gave out—I mean it gave out because we did not have any to start with—the train became bitterly cold, and we came near freezing and starving to death. That made our Russian experiences quite complete. We had foolishly started without even fruit, and there was nothing to be had on board the train except the tea which the conductors make in a samovar and serve to you at the slightest provocation. But even the tea was exhausted at last, and then the fire gave out, because all the wood had been used up.

There we were, penned up, wrapped in our seal-skins and steamer-rugs and with nubias over our heads, so cold that our teeth chattered, and so hungry we could have eaten anything. The conductor came and spoke to us several times, but whether he was inviting us to lunch or quoting Scripture we could never tell. There was no one on the train who spoke English or French, and nobody else in our car to speak anything at all—owing to our having come on this particular train, in order for my companion to "see Russia." I am delighted to record the fact that not only the outside but the inside windows were frosted so thickly that they had to light the sickly tallow candle in a tin box over the door of the compartment, so she never got a peep at Russia or anything else the whole way.

We consoled each other and kept up our spirits as best we could all day, but we arrived at Kiev so exhausted with cold and hunger that although we were received at the train by one of the most charming men I ever met, we both cried with relief at the sight of a friendly face and some one to whom we could speak and tell our woes. I have since wondered what he thought to be met by two forlorn women in tears! Whatever he thought, like all the Russians, he was courtesy itself, and we were soon whisked away to the inexpressible comfort of being thawed and fed.

Such a beautiful city as this is! Whitelaw Reid has declared Kiev to be one of the four picturesque cities in Europe; certainly it lies in a heavenly place, all up and down hills, with such vistas down the streets to where a mosque raises its gilded dome, or where an historic bronze statue stands out against the horizon. If Kiev had been planned by the French, it could not be more utterly beautiful. The domes of the cathedrals are blue, studded with gold stars; or else pale green or all gold, and the most exquisite churches in all Russia are in Kiev. A terrible monastery, where you take candles and go down into the bowels of the earth to see where monks martyred themselves, is here; and poor simple-minded pilgrims walk many hundred miles to kiss these tombs. Their devotion is pathetic. We had to walk in a procession of them, and I know that each of them had his own particular disease and his own special brand of dirt. The beggars surrounding the gate of this monastery are too awful to mention, yet it is reputed to be the richest monastery in all Russia.

In Kiev we heard "Hamlet" in Russian, and the man who played Hamlet was wonderfully good, surprisingly good. You don't know how strange it sounded to hear "To be or not to be" in Russian! The acting was so familiar, the words so strange. The audience went crazy over him, as Russian audiences always do. We watched him come out and bow thirty-nine times, and when we came away the noise was still deafening.

They make a sort of candy in Kiev which goes far and away above any sweets I ever have seen. It is a sort of candied rose. The whole rose is there. It is a solid soft pink mass, and it tastes just as a tea-rose smells. It is simply celestial.

We dearly love Kiev, it is so hauntingly beautiful. You can't forget it. Your mind keeps returning to it, but it is the sort of beauty that you can't describe satisfactorily. It is like your mother's face. You can see the beauty for yourself, but no one else can see it as you do, for the love which is behind it.

In Odessa we began to leave Russia behind us. Odessa is all sorts of a place. It is commercial, and not beautiful, but, as usual, our Russian friends made us forget the town and its sights, and remember only their sweet hospitality and friendliness.

We wished to catch the Russian steamer for Constantinople, but we were told that the police would not permit us to leave on such short notice. We felt that this was hard, for we had tried so consistently to be good in Russia that I was determined to go if possible. So I took an interpreter and drove to the police headquarters myself. To my amazement and delight my man told me that it could all be arranged by the payment of a few rubles. But that "few rubles" mounted up into many before I got my passports duly vised. I discovered that our American police are not so *very* different from Russian police after all, even if they *are* Irish!

We caught the steamer—the dear, clean, lovely *Nickolai II.*, with the stewardess a Greek named Aspasia, and I persisted in calling the steward Pericles, just to have things match.

Then we crunched our way out of the harbor through the ice into the Black Sea, and sailed away for Constantinople.

IX

CONSTANTINOPLE

Constantinople had three different effects upon me. The first was to make me utterly despise it for its sickening dirt; the second was when I forgot all about the mud and garbage, and went crazy over its picturesque streets with their steep slopes, odd turns, and bewitching vistas, and the last was to make me dread Cairo for fear it would seem tame in comparison, for Constantinople is enchanting. If I were a painter I would never leave off painting its delights and spreading its fascinations broadcast; and then I would take all the money I got for my pictures and spend it in the bazaars, and if I regretted my purchases I would barter them for others, because Constantinople is the beginning of the Orient, and if you remain long you become thoroughly metamorphosed, and you bargain, trade, exchange, and haggle until you forget that you ever were a Christian. The hour of our arrival in Constantinople was an accident. The steamer *Nickolai II.* was late, and as no one may land there after sunset, we were forced to lie in the Bosphorus all night.

It was dark when we sighted the city, but it was one of those clear darks where without any apparent light you can see everything. *Surely* no other city in the world has so beautiful an approach! Our great black steamer threaded her way between men-of-war, sail-boats, and all sorts of shipping, and if there were a thousand lights twinkling in the water there were a million from the city. It lies on a series of hills curved out like a monster amphitheatre, and it stretches all the way around. I looked up into the heavens, and it seemed to me that I never had seen so many stars in my life. Our sky at home has not so many. Yet there were no more than the yellow points of flame which flickered in every part of that sleeping city. Three tall minarets pierced above the horizon, and each of these wore circles of light which looked like necklaces and girdles of fire. Patches of black now and then showed where there were trees or marked a graveyard. Occasionally we heard a shrill cry or the barking of dogs, but these sounds came faintly, and seemed a part of the fairy-picture. It looked so much like a scene from an opera that I half expected to see the curtain go down and the lights flare up, and I feared the applause which always spoils the dream.

But nothing spoiled this dream. All night we lay in the beautiful Bosphorus, and all night at intervals I looked out of my porthole at that lovely sleeping princess. It never grew any less lovely. Its beauty and charm increased.

But in the morning everything was changed. A band of howling, screaming, roaring, fighting pirates came alongside in dirty row-boats, and to our utter consternation we found these bloodthirsty brigands were to row us to land. Not one word could we understand in all that fearful uproar. We were watching them in a terror too abject to describe, when, to our joy, an English voice said, "I am the guide for the two American ladies, and here is the kavass which the American minister sent down to meet you. The consul at Odessa cabled your arrival."

Oh, how glad we were! We loaded them with thanks and hand-luggage, and scrambled down the stairway at the side of the steamer. A dozen dirty hands were stretched out to receive us. We clutched at their sleeves instead, and pitched into the boat, and our trunks came tumbling after us, and away we went over the roughest of seas, which splashed us and made us feel a little queer; and then we landed at the dirtiest, smelliest quay, and picked our way through a filthy custom-house, where, in spite of bribery and corruption, they opened my trunk and examined all the photographs of the family, which happened to be on top, and made remarks about them in Turkish which made the other men laugh. The mud came up over our overshoes as we stood there, so that altogether we were quite heated in temper when we found ourselves in an alley outside, filled with garbage which had been there forever, and learned that this alley was a street, and a very good one for Constantinople, too.

The porters in Turkey are marvels of strength. They wear a sort of cushioned saddle on their backs, and to my amazement two men tossed my enormous trunk on this saddle. I saw it leave their hands before it reached his poor bent back; he staggered a little, gave it a hitch to make it more secure, then started up the hill on a trot.

I never saw so much mud, such unspeakably filthy streets, and so many dogs as Constantinople can boast. You drive at a gallop up streets slanting at an angle of forty-five degrees, and you nearly fall out of the back of the carriage. Then presently you come to the top of that hill and start down the other side, still at a gallop, and you brace your feet to keep from pitching over the driver's head. You would notice the dogs first were it not for the smells. But as it is, you cannot even see until you get your salts to your nose. The odors are so thick that they darken the air. You are disappointed in the dogs, however. There are quite as many of them as you expected. You have not been misled as to the number of them, but nowhere have I seen them described in a satisfactory way—so that you knew what to expect, I mean. In the first place, they hardly look like dogs. They have woolly tails like sheep. Their eyes are dull, sleepy, and utterly devoid of expression. Constantinople dogs have neither masters nor brains. No brains because no masters. Perhaps no masters because no brains. Nobody wants to adopt an idiot. They are, of course, mongrels of the most hopeless type. They are yellowish, with thick, short, woolly coats, and much fatter than you expect to find them. They walk like a funeral procession. Never have I seen one frisk or even wag his tail. Everybody turns out for them. They sleep—from twelve to twenty of them—on a single pile of garbage, and never notice either men or each other unless a dog which lives in the next street trespasses. Then they eat him up, for they are jackals as well as dogs, and they are no more epicures than ostriches. They never show interest in anything. They are *blase*. I saw some mother dogs asleep, with tiny puppies swarming over them like little fat rats, but the mothers paid no attention to them. Children seem to bore them quite as successfully as if they were women of fashion.

We went sailing up the Golden Horn to the Skutari cemetery, one of the loveliest spots of this thrice-fascinating Constantinople. As we were descending that steep hill upon which it is situated we met a darling little baby Turk in a fez riding on a pony which his father was leading. This child of a different race, and six thousand miles away, looked so much like our Billy that I wanted to eat him up—dirt and all. I contented myself with giving him backsheesh, while my companion photographed him. Such an afternoon as that was on that lovely golden river, with the sun just setting, and our picturesque boatmen sending the boat through thousands upon thousands of sea-gulls just to make them fly, until the air grew dark with their wings, and the sunlight on their white breasts looked like a great glistening snow-storm!

One night we went to a masked ball given for the benefit of a new hospital which is situated upon the Golden Horn. It was given by Mr. Levy, one of the Turkish Commissioners at the World's Fair, and the decorations were something marvellous. The walls were hung with embroideries which drove us the next day to the bazaars and nearly bankrupted us. Every street of Constantinople looks like a masked ball, so this one merely continued the illusion. We could distinguish the Mohammedan women from the others because they all went home before midnight without unmasking.

This ball is interesting because it is called "The Engagement Ball." We were told that only at a subscription ball given for a charity in which their parents are interested and feel under moral obligation to support by their presence are the young people of Constantinople allowed to meet each other. The fathers and mothers occupy the boxes, and thus, under their very eyes, and masked, can love affairs be brought to a conclusion. During the week which followed no fewer than ten important engagements were duly heralded in the columns of the newspapers.

The most exciting things in Constantinople are the earthquakes. We were afraid they would not have any while we were there, but they accommodated us with a very satisfactory one! It upset my ink-bottle and broke the lamp and rattled everything in the room until I was delighted. When my companion came in she was indignant to think that I had enjoyed the earthquake all to myself, for she was in the rooms of the American Bible Society, and being thus protected, did not feel it. But I told her that that was her punishment for trying to prove that a missionary had cheated her, for she was not in that place for a godly purpose.

At another time, however, we met with better success in

obtaining a sensation of a different sort. We visited, in company with our Turkish friend, a small but wonderfully beautiful mosque not often seen by ordinary tourists, and afterwards went up on Galata tower to get the fine view of Constantinople which may be had there. It was just before sunset again, and I am quite unable to make you see the utter loveliness of it. We crawled out on the narrow ledge which surrounds the top, and I had just got a capital picture of my companion as she clutched the Turk to prevent being blown off, for the wind was something terrible, when suddenly the keepers rushed to the windows and jabbered excitedly in Turkish and ran up a flag, and behold, there was a fire! Galata tower is the fire observatory. By the flags they hoist you can tell where the fire is. I never was at a fire in my life. Even when our stables burned down I was away from home. So here was my opportunity. The way we drove down those narrow streets was enough to make one think that we were the fire department itself. But when we arrived we found to our grief that it was our dear little mosque which was burning. Undoubtedly we were the last visitors to enter it.

We went back to the hotel for dinner, and about nine o'clock, hearing that the fire was spreading, we drove down again with our Turk, who regarded it as no unusual thing to take American women to two fires in the same day. We found the tenement-houses burning. Our carriage gave us no vantage-ground, so our friend, who speaks twelve languages, obtained permission to enter a house and go up on the roof. We never stopped to think that we might catch all sorts of diseases; we were so pleased at the courtesy of the poor souls. They had all their poor belongings packed ready to remove if the fire crept any nearer, but they ran ahead and lighted us up the dark stairway with candles, and told us in Turkish what an honor we were doing their house, all of which touched me deeply. I wondered how many people I would have assisted up to *our* roof if *my* clothes were tied up in sheets in the hall, with the fire not a square away!

Fortunately, it came no nearer, and from that high, flat roof we watched the seething mass of yellow flames grow less and less and then go completely under control. It was Providence which did it, however, and not the Constantinople fire department, with its little streams of water the size of slate-pencils!

The dogs were one of the sights we were anxious to see; the Sultan was the other. We found the bazaars more fascinating than either. But we wanted to photograph the Sultan—chiefly, I think, because it was forbidden. I have an ever-present unruly desire to do everything which these foreign countries absolutely forbid. But everybody said we could not. So we very meekly went to see him go to prayers, and left our cameras with the kavass. We had, with our customary good fortune, a window directly in front of the Sultan's gate, not twenty feet from the door of the mosque.

"If I had that camera here I could get him, and *nobody* would know!" I declared.

"But there are so many spies," our Turkish friend said. "It would be too dangerous."

We waited, and waited, and waited. Never have the hours seemed so mortally long as they seemed to us as we watched the hands of the clock crawl past luncheon-time, hours and hours later than the Sultan was announced to pray, and still no Sultan. His little six-and seven-year old sons, in the uniform of colonels, were mounted on superb Arabian horses. These horses had tails so long that servants held them up going through the mud, as if they were ladies' trains. The children were dear things, with clear olive complexions and soft, dark eyes—Italian eyes. Then they grew tired of waiting, and dismounted, and came up to where we were, and shook hands in the sweetest manner. My companion was for coaxing the little one into her lap, but she looked somewhat staggered when I reminded her that she would be trotting the colonel of the regiment on her knee.

Then more cavalry came, and more bands, playing a little the worst of any that I ever heard, and we impatiently thrust our heads out of the window, thinking, of course, the Sultan was coining, but he was not. Then some infantry with white leggings and stiff knee-joints, with coils of green gas-pipe on their heads, like our student-lamps, marched by with a gait like a battalion of horses with the string-halt, and we shrieked with laughter. Our friend said they called that the German step. Germany would declare war with Turkey if she ever heard that.

By this time we were so tired and hungry and disgusted that we were about to go home and give up the Sultan when we saw no fewer than fifty men come toiling up the hill with carpet-bags, as if they had brought their clothes, and intended to see the Sultan if it took a week. I do not know who or what they were, and I do not want to know. They served their purpose with us in that they put us into instantaneous good humor, and just then there was a commotion, and everybody straightened up and craned their necks; and then, preceded by his body-guard, the Sultan drove slowly down, looked directly up at our window (and we groaned), and then turned in at the gate. Opposite to him sat Osman Pasha, the hero of Plevna. The ladies of the harem were driven into the court-yard surrounded by eunuchs, the horses were taken from their carriages, and there the ladies sat, guarded like prisoners, until the Sultan came out again. He then mounted into a superb gold chariot drawn by two beautiful white horses, and he himself drove out. Everybody salaamed, and he raised his hand in return as if it was all the

Lilian Bell

greatest possible bore.

While he was driving into the court-yard the priest came out on the minaret and called men to prayer, and an English girl who sat at the next window informed her mother that he was announcing the names of the important persons in the procession! Her mother trained her glasses on him—a mere speck against the sky—and said, "Fancy!"

The Sultan is not a beauty. If he were in America his sign would be that of the three golden balls.

We went to see the mosques, and the officials and priests and boatmen were so cross and surly on account of the fast of Ramazan that they would not let us take photographs without a fight. During Ramazan they neither eat nor drink between sunrise and sunset.

On the fifteenth day of Ramazan the Sultan goes to the mosque of Eyoob to buckle on the sword of Mohammed in order to remind himself that the power of that sword has descended to himself. He does not announce his route, therefore the whole city is in a commotion, and they spread miles of streets with sand for fear he might take it into his head to go by some unusual way. It passes my comprehension why they should ever put any more dirt in the streets even for a Sultan. But sand is a mark of respect in Russia and Turkey, and it really cleans the streets a little. At least it absorbs the mud. Just as we were about to start for a balcony beneath which he was almost sure to pass, our Turkish friend whispered to us that if we wore capes we might take our cameras. Imagine our delight, for it was so dangerous. But the capes! Ours were not half long enough to conceal the camera properly. It was growing late. So in a perfect frenzy I dragged out my long pale blue *sortie du bal*, ripped the white velvet capes from it, pinned a short sable cape to the top of it with safety-pins, and enveloped myself in this gorgeousness at eleven o'clock in the morning. We made a curious trio. Our Turk was in English tweeds with a fez. My companion wore a smart tailor gown, and I was got up as if for a fancy-dress ball, but in the streets of Constantinople no one gave me a second glance. I was in mourning compared to some of the others.

On the balcony with us were two small boys with projecting ears, of whom I stood in deadly terror, for if their boyish interest centred in that camera of mine I was lost. Presently, however, with a tremendous clatter, the Sultan's advance-guard came galloping down the street. I got them, turned the film, and was ready for the next—the carriages of the state officials. I aimed well, and got them, but I was growing nervous. The boys writhed closer. I shoved them a little when their mother was not looking.

"Don't try to take so many," said our Turk. "Here comes the Sultan. Aim low, and don't fire until you see the whites of his eyes."

Again he looked up directly at us, and I snapped the shutter promptly. It was done. I had succeeded in photographing the Sultan! To be sure, it was an offense against the state, punishable by fine and imprisonment, but nobody had caught me. The little boy next to me, who had walked on my dress and ground his elbows into me, craned his neck and stared at the Sultan with round eyes. He had been in my way ever since we arrived, but in an exuberance of tenderness I patted his head.

But when we had those negatives developed I discovered to my disgust that instead of the Sultan I had taken an excellent photograph of that wretched little boy's ear.

X

CAIRO

I need not have been afraid that the charms of Constantinople would spoil Cairo for me, although at first I was disappointed. Most places have to be lived up to, especially one like Cairo, whose attractions are vaunted by every tourist, every woman of fashion, every scholar, every idle club-man, everybody, either with brains or without. I wondered how it *could* be all things to all men. I simply thought it was the fashion to rave about it, and I was sick of the very sound of its name before I came. It was too perfect. It aroused the spirit of antagonism in me.

First of all, when you arrive in Cairo you find that it is very, very fashionable. You can get everything here, and yet it is practically the end of the world. Nearly everybody who comes here turns around and goes back. Few go on. Even when you go up the Nile you must come back to Cairo. There is really nowhere else to go.

You drive through smart English streets, and when you find yourself at Shepheard's you are at the most famous hotel in the world; yet, strange to say, in spite of its size, in spite of the thousands of learned, famous, titled, and distinguished people who have been here, in spite of its smartness and fashion, it is the most homelike hotel I ever was in. Everybody seems to know about you and to take an interest in what you are doing, and all the servants know your name and the number of your room, and when you go out into the great corridor, or when you sit on the terrace, there is not a trace of the supercilious scrutiny which takes a mental inventory of your clothes and your looks and your letter of credit, which so often spoils the sunset for you at similar hotels.

Ghezireh Palace is even more fashionable than Shepheard's. Here we have baronets and counts and a few earls. But there they have dukes and kings and emperors, yet there is a gold-and-alabaster mantelpiece which takes your mind even from royalty, it is so beautiful. Ghezireh is situated on the Nile, half an hour's drive away, so that in spite of its royal atmosphere it never will take the place of Shepheard's. Here you see all the interesting people you have heard of in your life. You trip over the easels of famous artists in an angle of the narrow street, and many famous authors, scientists, archaeologists, and scholars are here working or resting.

Yesterday I was told that four Americans who stood talking together on the terrace represented two hundred millions of dollars. At dinner the red coats of the officers make brilliant spots of color among all the black of the other men, and at first sight it does seem too odd to see evening dress consist of black trousers and a bright-red coat which stops off short at the waist. But if you think that looks odd, what will you say to the officers of the Highland regiments? *Their* full dress is almost as immodest in a different way as that of some women, and one of the most exquisite paradoxes of British custom is that a Highland undress uniform consists of the addition of long-trousers—more clothes than they wear in dress uniform.

Cairo is cosmopolitan. You may ride a smart cob, a camel, or a donkey, and nobody will even look twice at you. You will see harem carriages with closed blinds; coupes with the syces running before them (and there is nothing in Cairo more beautiful than some of these men and the way they run); you will see the Khedive driving with his body-guard of cavalry; you will see fat Egyptian nurses out in basket phaeton with little English children; you will see tiny boys, no bigger than our Billy, in a fever of delight over riding on a live donkey, and attended by a syce; you will see emancipated Egyptian women trying to imitate European dress and manners, and making a mess of it; you will see gamblers, adventurers, and savants all mixed together, with all the hues of the rainbow in their costumes; you will see water-carriers carrying drinking-water in nasty-looking dried skins, which still retain the outlines of the animals, only swollen out of shape, and unspeakably revolting; you will see native women carrying their babies astride their shoulders, with the little things resting their tiny brown hands on their mothers' heads, and often laying their little black heads down, too, and going fast to sleep, while these women walk majestically through the streets with only their eyes showing; you will see all sorts of hideous cripples, and more blind and cross-eyed people than you ever saw in all your life before; you will see venders of fly-brushes, turquoises, amber, ostrich-feathers, bead necklaces from Nubia, scarabaei and antiquities which bear the hall-marks of the manufacturers as clearly as if stamped "Made in Germany"; you will see sore-eyed children sitting in groups in doorways, with numberless flies on each eye, making no effort to dislodge them; and you will visit mosques and bazaars which you feel sure call for insect-powder; you will see Arabian men knitting stockings in the street, and thinking it no shame; you will see countless eunuchs with their coal-black, beardless faces, their long, soft, nerveless hands, long legs, and the general make-up of a mushroom-boy who has outgrown his strength; you will hear the cawing of countless rooks and crows, and if you leave your window open these rascals will fly in and eat your fruit and sweets; you will see and hear the picturesque lemonade-vendor selling his vile-tasting acid from a long, beautiful brass vessel of irregular shape, and you never can get away from the horrible jangling noise he makes from two brass bowls to call attention to his wares; you will see tiny boys in tights doing acrobatic feats on the sidewalk, walking on their hands in front of you for a whole square as you take your afternoon stroll, and then pleading with you for backsheesh; you will see hideous monkeys of a sort you never saw before, trained to do the same thing, so that you cannot walk out in Cairo without being attended with some sort of a bodyguard, either monkey, acrobat, cripple, or the beggar-girls with their sweet, plaintive voices, their pretty smiles, and their eternal hunger, to coax the piasters from your open purse. But you accept these sights and sounds as a part of this wonderful old city, and each day the fascination will grow on you until you will be obliged to go to a series of afternoon teas in order to cool your enthusiasm.

In passing, the flies of Egypt deserve a tribute to their peculiar qualities. A plague of American flies would be a luxury compared to the visit of one fly from Egypt. For untold centuries they have been in the habit of crawling over thick-skinned faces and bodies, and not being dislodged. They can stay all day if they like. Consequently, if they see an American eye, and they light on it, not content with that, they try to crawl in. You attempt to brush them off, but they only move around to the other side, until you nearly go mad with nervousness from their sticky feet. If they find out your ear they crawl in and walk around. You cannot discourage them. They craze you with their infuriating persistence. If *I* had been the Egyptians, the Israelites would have been escorted out of the country in state at the arrival of the first fly.

England has done a marvellous good to Egypt by her training. She has taken a lot of worthless rascals and educated them to work at something, no matter if it does take five of them to call a cab. She has trained them to make good soldiers, well drilled because drilled by English officers, and making a creditable showing. She has made fairly dependable policemen of them, but their legs are the most wabbly and crooked of any that ever were seen. These policemen are armed. One carries a pistol and the other the cartridges. If they happened to be together they could be very dangerous to criminals. She has developed all the resources of the country, and made it fat and productive, but she never can give the common people brains.

It poured rain this morning, and there is no drainage; consequently, rivers of water were rushing down the gutters, making crossings impassable and traffic impossible. They called out the fire-engines to pump the water up in the main thoroughfare, but on a side street I stopped the carriage for half an hour and watched four Arabs working at the problem. One walked in with a broom and swept the water down the gutter to another man who had a dust-pan. With this dustpan he scooped up as much as a pint of water at a time, and poured it into a tin pail, which gave occupation to the third Arab, who stood in a bent position and urged him on. The fourth Arab then took this pail of water, ran out, and emptied it into the middle of the street, and the water beat him running back to the gutter. I said to them, "Why don't you use a sieve? It would take longer." And they said, "No speak English."

I watched them until I grew tired, and then I went to the ostrich-farm as a sort of distraction, and I really think that an ostrich has more brains than an Arab.

This farm is very large, and the ostrich-pens are built of mud. I never had seen ostriches before, and I had no idea how hideous, how big, and how enchanting they are. They have the most curious agate-colored eyes—colorless, cold, yet intelligent eyes. But they are the eyes of a bird without a conscience. They have no soul, as camels have. An ostrich looks as if he would really enjoy villainy, as if he could commit crime after crime from pure love of it, and never know remorse; yet there is a fascination about the old birds, and they have their good points. The father is domestic in spite of looking as if he belonged to all the clubs, and, much to my delight, I saw one sitting on the eggs while the mother walked out and took the air. Ostriches and Arabs do women's work with an admirable disregard of Mrs. Grundy. Ostriches have an irresistible way of waving their lovely plumy wings, and one old fellow twenty-five years old actually imitates the dervishes. The keeper says to him, "Dance," and although he is about ten feet tall, he sits down with his scaly legs spread out on each side of him, and, shutting his eyes, he throws his long, ugly red neck from side to side, making a curious grunting noise, and waving his wings in billowy line like a skirt-dancer. It was too wonderful to see him, and it was almost as revolting as a real dervish.

We saw these dervishes once; nothing could persuade us to go twice—they were too nasty. The night the Khedive goes to the Citadel, to the mosque of Mohammed Ali, to pray for his heart's desire (for on that night all prayers of the faithful are sure to be answered), the dervishes in great numbers are performing their rites. They are called the howling dervishes, but they do not howl; they only make a horrible grunting noise. They have long, dirty, greasy hair, and as they throw their bodies backward and forward this hair flies, and sometimes strikes the careless observer in the face. They work themselves up to a perfect passion of religious ecstasy to the monotonous sound of Arab music, and never have I heard or seen anything more revolting. The negroes in the South when they "get the power" are not nearly so repulsive.

It is England's wise policy in all her colonies to have her army take part in the national religious ceremonies, so when the Sacred Carpet started from the Citadel on its journey to Mecca there was a magnificent military display.

It is an odd thing to call it a carpet, for it not only is not a carpet in itself, but it is not the shape of a carpet, it is not used for a carpet, and does not look like a carpet.

We were among the fortunate ones who were invited to the private view of it the night before, when the faithful were dedicating it. They sat on the floor, these Mohammedans, rocking themselves back and forth, and chanting the Koran. I believe the reason nearly all Arabs have crooked legs is because they squat so much. One cannot have straight legs when one uses one's legs to sit down on for hours at a time. They always sit in the sun, too, and that must bake them into their crookedness.

The "carpet" is a black velvet embroidered solidly in silver and gold. It is shaped like an old-fashioned Methodist church, only there are minarets at the four corners. It looks like a pall. Every year they send a new one to Mecca, and then the old one is cut into tiny bits and distributed among the faithful, who wear it next their hearts.

This carpet was about six feet long, and was railed in so that no one could touch it. A man stood by and sprayed attar of roses on you as you passed, but I do not know what he did it for, unless it was to turn sensitive women faint with the heaviness of the perfume.

But the next morning the procession formed, and amid the

wildest enthusiasm, the bowing and salaaming of the men, and the shouting and running of the children, and the singing of the Arabs who bore the carpet, it was placed upon the most magnificent camel I ever saw, which was covered from head to foot with cloth of gold, and whose very gait seemed more majestic because of his sacred burden, and thus, led by scores of enthusiastic Arabs, he moved slowly down the street, following the covering for the tomb, and in turn being followed by one scarcely less magnificent destined to cover the sacred carpet in its camel journey to Mecca. That was absolutely all there was to it, yet the Khedive was there with a fine military escort, and all Cairo turned out at the unearthly hour of eight o'clock in the morning to see it.

As we drove back we saw the streets for blocks around a certain house hung with colored-glass lanterns, and thousands upon thousands of small Turkey-red banners with white Arabic letters on them strung on wires on each side of the street. These we knew were the decorations for the famous wedding which was to occur that night, and to which we had fortunately been bidden. It was in very smart society. The son of a pasha was to marry the daughter of a pasha, and the presents were said to be superb.

We wore our best clothes. We had ordered our bouquets beforehand, for one always presents the bride with a bouquet, and they were really very beautiful. It was a warm night, with no wind, and the heavens were twinkling with millions of stars. Such big stars as they have in Egypt!

When we arrived we were taken in charge by a eunuch so black that I had to feel my way up-stairs. There were, perhaps, fifty other eunuchs standing guard in the ante-chamber, and our dragoman took the men who brought us around to another door, where all the men had to wait while we women visited the bride.

A motley throng of women were in the outer room—fat black women with waists two yards around, canary-colored women laced into low-cut European evening dresses, brown women in native dress; a babel of voices, chattering in curious French, Arabic, Turkish, and Greek. All the women were terribly out of shape from every point of view, and not a pretty one among them. One attendant snatched my bouquet without even a "Thank you" (I had been wondering to whom I should give it, but I need not have worried), and patted me on the back as she pushed me into the room where the bride sat on a throne amid piles upon piles of bouquets. She had a heavy, pale face covered with powder, eyes and eyebrows blackened, nails stained with henna, and a figure much too fat. She wore a garment made of something which looked like mosquito-netting heavily embroidered in gold, which hung like a rag. Her jewels were magnificent, but the effect of all this gorgeousness was rather spoiled to the artistic eye by her grotesque surroundings.

After we had visited the bride we were approached by a little yellow woman in blue satin, who asked me in French if I would not like to see the *chambre a coucher*, and I said I would. We were then conducted to a room all hung in blue satin embroidered in red. Lambrequins, chair-covers, bed-covers, pillows, bed-hangings—all the careful work of the bride. Then we were invited to inspect the presents in another room, which were all in glass cabinets. Dozens of amber and jewelled cigarette-holders and ornaments of every description, most magnificent, but of no earthly use—as wedding presents sometimes are.

Then we came down-stairs, and had all sorts of things at a banquet, and heard Arab music, and sat around in the room, where our men met us, and feeling rather bored, we decided to go home. There we were wise, for we met quite by accident the procession of the bridegroom. He was escorted through the streets by a band, and two rows of young men carrying candelabra under glass shades. We turned and drove along beside him and watched him, but he was so nervous we felt that it was rather a mean thing to do. He was a handsome fellow, but never have I seen a man who looked so unhappy and ill at ease. When he entered the house he proceeded to the door of the bride's room, where he threw down silver and gold as backsheesh until her women were satisfied; then he was permitted to enter.

As we drove away for the second time I remembered that they were having "torchlight tattoo" at the barracks, and we decided to stop for a moment.

"It won't seem bad to see some soldiers who can march, for the English soldiers are magnificently trained," I said, as we stopped to buy our tickets. A young officer whom I had met heard my remark, and smiled and saluted.

"The English soldiers *are* the best in the world, *aren't* they?" he said, teasingly.

"Undoubtedly," I replied, tranquilly.

He looked a little staggered. He had encountered my belligerent spirit before, and he did not expect me to agree with him.

"You—you, an American, admit *that*?" he said.

"Surely," I replied. "But why?" he persisted, most unwisely, for it gave me my chance.

"Because the Americans are the only ones who ever whipped them! American soldiers can beat even the best!"

It is now six weeks since I said that, but as yet he has made
no reply.

XI

THE NILE

In travelling abroad there are some things which you wish to do more than others. There are certain treasures you particularly desire to see, certain scenes your mind has pictured, until the dream has almost become a reality. The ascent of the Nile was one of my Meccas, and now that it is over the reality has almost become a dream.

In Egypt the weather is so nearly perfect during the season that it was no surprise to find the day of our departure a cloudless one. I seldom worry myself to arrange beforehand for the creature comforts of a journey, trusting to the beneficent star which seems to hover over the unworthy to shine upon my pathway. But this time I had so dreamed of and brooded over and longed for the Nile that I went so far as to investigate the different lines of boats, and we chose the moonlight time of the month, and we hurried through Russia and Turkey and Greece with but one aim in view, and that was to have our feet on the deck of the *Mayflower* on the 19th of February. And we succeeded.

Ah, it was a dream well worth realizing! Twenty-one days of rest. Three glorious weeks of smooth sailing over calm waters. Three weeks of warmth and sunshine by day, and of poetry and starlight by night. Three weeks of drifting in the romance which surrounds the name of that great sorceress, that wonderful siren, that consummate coquette, that most fascinating woman the world has ever known. Three weeks of steeping one's soul in the oldest, most complete and satisfactory ruins on the face of the earth. Here, in delving into the past, we would have no use for the comparative word "hundreds." We could boldly use the superlative word "thousands." What memories! what dreams! what fragments of half-forgotten history and romance came floating through the brain! I have, generally, little use for guide-books except, afterwards, to verify what I have seen. But I admit that I had an especial longing to reach the temple of Denderah, which was said to contain the most famous relief of Cleopatra extant. I was anxious to see if her beauty or her charm or anything which accounted for her sorceries were reproduced. "If Cleopatra's nose had been shorter, the whole history of the world would have been changed." How far away she seemed! How near she would become!

On the terrace at Shepheard's the morning of our departure you could see by people's faces how they were going to make this journey. Some had Stanley helmets on, and were laden with cushions and steamer-chairs and fruits as if for an ocean voyage. Others were clutching their Baedeker, and their Amelia Edwards, and their "Kismet," and their note-books, and wore a do-or-die expression of countenance. One or two others floated around aimlessly, with dreamy eyes, as if they were already lost in the past which now pressed so closely at hand. Then the coach from the Gehzireh Palace rolled by in a cloud of dust, and people hurried down the steps of Shepheard's and took their places in *our* coach, and the dragomans in their gorgeous costumes followed with wraps, and the porters bustled about stowing away hand-luggage, and Arabs crowded near, thrusting their violets and roses and amber necklaces and beaded fly-brushes into your very face, and the old man who sells turquoises made his last effort to sell you a set for shirt-studs, and the Egyptians and East-Indians from the bazaars opposite came to the door and looked on with the perennial interest and friendliness of the Orient, and a swarm of beggars pleaded, with the excitement of a last chance, for backsheesh, and there was a babel of tongues—French, English, Italian, German, and Arabic, all hurtling about your ears like so many verbal bullets in a battle, when suddenly the door slammed, the driver cracked his whip, the coach lurched forward, the children scattered— and we were off.

Everybody knows when a boat starts up the Nile, and everybody is interested and nods and waves to everybody else. There was a short drive to the river amid polite calls of "good-bye" and "*bon voyage*," and there lay the *Mayflower*, like a great white bird with comfortably folded wings. Nobody seemed to hurry much, for a Nile boat does not start until her passengers are all on board. An hour or so makes no difference.

You go down the bank of the Nile to go on board a boat upon steps cut in the earth, and if your hands are full and you cannot hold up your dress, you sweep some three inches of fine yellow dust after you. But you don't care. The man ahead scuffed his dust in your face, and the woman behind you is sneezing in yours, and everything and everybody are a little yellowish from it, but nobody stops to brush it off. It is too exciting to hurry up on deck and place your steamer-chair and fling your things into your stateroom and rush out again for fear that you will miss something. There were Italians, French, English, Poles, Swedes, and Americans on board. Some of them had titles. Some had only bad manners, with nothing to excuse them. But, after all, everybody was nice, I got through the whole three weeks without hating anybody and with only wanting to drown one passenger.

What better record of amiability could you ask?

But one thing marred the start. This Anglo-American line of boats is the only line in Egypt which flies the American flag. That was the final inducement they offered which decided my choice of the *Mayflower*. But while we knew that she was obliged to fly the British flag also, we were indignant beyond words to see a huge Union Jack floating at the top of the forward flagstaff and beneath it a toy American flag about the size of a cigar-box. *Beneath* the English flag! I nearly wept with rage. The owner of the line was at hand, and I did not wait to draw up a petition or to consult my fellow-Americans. I just said: "Have the goodness to haul down that infant American flag, will you? I have no objection to sailing under both, but I do object to such an insulting disparity in size. Besides that, you seem to have forgotten that the American flag never flies *below* any other flag on God's green earth!"

He made some apologies, and gave the order at once. The baby was hauled down amid the smiles of the English passengers. But at Assiout we were avenged when an enormous American flag arrived by rail and was hoisted to the main flagstaff, twenty feet higher than the British. When I came out on deck that Sunday morning, and saw that blessed flag waving above me, everything blurred before my eyes, and I do assure you that it was the most beautiful sight I saw in all of that European continent. You may talk about your temples and your ruins and your old masters! Have *you* ever seen "Old Glory" flying straight out from a flagstaff in a foreign country seven thousand miles away from home?

The Nile is much broader than I expected to find it, and, like the Missouri and the Golden Horn, it is always muddy. The *Mayflower* carries only fifty passengers, which is of the greatest advantage for donkey-rides and for seeing the ruins, a larger party being unwieldy. She draws but two feet of water, having been built expressly for Nile service, so we had the proud satisfaction of seeing one of the big Rameses boats stuck on a sand-bank for eighteen hours, while we tooted past her blowing whistles of defiance and derision. Whenever we felt ourselves going aground on a sand-bank we just reversed the engines and backed off again, or else put on extra steam and ground our way through it. In the whole three weeks we were not aground five minutes, although we passed one wreck settling in the water, with the bedding and stores piled up on the bank, and the passengers sailing away in the swallow-winged feluccas, which had swooped down to their rescue like so many compassionate birds.

Afternoon tea on the Nile is an unforgetable function. Everybody comes on deck and sits under the awning and watches the sun go down. Each day the sunsets grow more beautiful. Each day they differ from all the rest. Such yellows and purples! Such violet shadows on the golden water! Such a marvellously sudden sinking of the sun in a crimson flame behind the flat brown hills! And then the stillness of the Nile in the opal aftermath! Those sunsets are something to carry in the memory forever and a day.

At night the sailors lower the side awnings, crawling along the railings with their naked prehensile feet. The captain, a Nubian, on a salary of eighty-five cents a day, selects a suitable spot on the bank where the boat may remain all night. Then the bow of the boat heads for the shore and digs her nose in the soft mud. The sailors pitch the stakes and mallets out on to the bank and spring ashore. Then with Arab songs which they always sing when rowing, hauling ropes, scrubbing the decks, or doing any sort of work, the stern is gradually hauled alongside the bank, and there we stay until morning in a stillness so absolute that even the cry of the jackals seems in harmony with the loneliness of it.

Lilian Bell

I dreaded the first excursion. It was to Memphis and Sakhara, eighteen miles in all, and I never had been on a donkey in my life. I am not afraid of horses, but donkeys are so much like mules. My friends encouraged me all they could. They said that I would have a donkey-boy all to myself, that the donkey never went out of a walk, and wound up by the cheerful assurance that if he did pitch me over his head I would not have far to fall.

The donkey-boys of the Nile deserve a book all to themselves. Such craft! Such flattery! Such knowledge of human nature! With unerring sagacity they discover your nationality and give your donkey names famous in your own country. Never will an Englishman find himself astride "Yankee Doodle" or "Uncle Sam," or an American upon "John Bull." They pick you up in their arms to put you on or take you from your donkey as if you were a baby. They run beside you holding your umbrella with one hand, and with the other arm holding you on if you are timid. Staid, dignified women who teach Sunday-school classes at home, who would not permit a white manservant to touch them, lean on their donkey-boys as if they were human balustrades.

My first donkey-boy was an enchanting rascal. He looked like a handsome bronze statue. My donkey was a pale, drab little beast, woolly and dejected. He looked as though if you hurled contemptuous epithets at him for a week they would all fit his case. My companion's was more jaunty. He had been clipped in patterns. His legs were all done in hieroglyphics, and he held his ears up while mine trailed his in the sand.

Nevertheless, I was so deadly afraid of him that I saw my forty-nine fellow-passengers leave me, one after the other, while I still hesitated and eyed him suspiciously. Perhaps I never would have mounted had not Imam, the dragoman, with the frank unceremoniousness of the East, caught me up in his arms and landed me on my donkey before I could protest. And in the face of his childish smile of confidence I could only gasp. We moved off with the majesty of a funeral procession.

"What's the name of my donkey?" asked my companion.

"Cleveland," came the answer like a flash.

We were enchanted.

"And what's the name of mine?" I asked.

"McKinley!"

Then we shouted. You have no idea how funny it sounded to hear those two familiar names in such strange surroundings. We nearly tumbled off in our delight, and so quick are those clever little donkey-boys to watch your face and divine your mood that in a second they gave that Weird, long-drawn donkey call, "Oh-h-ah-h!" and my companion's donkey swung into a gentle trot, with her donkey-boy running behind, beating him with a stick and pinching him in the legs.

At that McKinley, not to be outdone by any Democratic donkey, pricked up his ears. I heard a terrific commotion behind me. The string of bells around McKinley's neck deafened me, and I remember then and there losing all confidence in the administration, for McKinley was a Derby winner. He was a circus donkey. He broke into a crazy gallop, then into a mad run. I shrieked but my donkey-boy thought it was a sound of joy, and only prodded him the more. In less than two minutes I had shot past every one of the party; and for the whole day McKinley and I headed the procession. I only saw my companion at a distance through a cloud of dust, and she does not trust me any more. Thus have I to bear the sins of Mohammed Ali, my perfidious donkey-boy, who forced me to lead the van on that dreadful first day at Sakhara.

Everywhere you go you hear the insistent, importunate cry for backsheesh. Old men, women, children, dragomans, guides, merchants, and street-venders—all sorts and conditions of men beg for it. They teach even babies to take hold of your dress and cry for it. And to toss backsheesh over to the crowd on the bank as the steamer moves away is to see every one of them roll over in the dirt and fight and scratch like cats over half a piaster. There is no such thing as self-respect among the natives. They are governed by blows and curses, and even the eyes of sheiks and native police glisten at the word "backsheesh."

At Assiout one night we heard some one calling from the bank in English: "Lady, lady, give me some English books. I am a Christian. I can read English. Give me a Bible. I go to the American college. I want to be a preacher." I leaned over the railing and discerned a very black boy, whose name, he said, was Solomon. I was so surprised to hear "Bible" instead of "backsheesh" that I investigated. He said his mother and father were dead; that he had only been to college a year; that he wanted to be a preacher, and that he would pray God for me if I would give him a Bible. I was touched. He spelled America, and I gave him backsheesh. He told me the population of the United States, and I gave him more backsheesh. He sang "Upidee" with an accent which threw me into such ecstasies that it brought the whole boat to hear him, and we all gave him backsheesh. But his piety was what captivated us. I heard afterwards that no fewer than ten of us privately resolved to give him Bibles. He begged us to visit the college; so the next day eight of us gave up the tombs and went to the American college, which was floating the Stars and Stripes because it was Washington's birthday. We spoke to Dr. Alexander, the president, of our friend Solomon. He told us that he was an absolute fraud, but one of the cleverest boys in the college. He was not an orphan. His father took a new wife every year, and his mother also had an assorted collection of husbands. He had been to school five years instead of one. He had no end of Bibles. People gave them to him and he sold them. He had been in jail for stealing, and on the whole his showing was not such as to encourage us to help him to preach. Such was Solomon, a typical Egyptian, an equally accurate type of the Arab. They are the cleverest and most consummate liars in the world. I wonder that the noble men and women who are giving their lives to teaching in that wonderful mission college have the courage to go on with it, the material is so unpromising. Yet Arabic acuteness makes it interesting, after all. A pretty little water-carrier named Fatima, who wore a blue bead in the hole bored in her nose, and only one other garment besides, ran beside me at Denderah, calling me "beautiful princess," and kissing my hand until she made my glove sticky. None of us were too old or too hideous in our Nile costumes to be called beautiful and good. My donkey-boy at Karnak assured me that I was his father and his mother. He touched his forehead to my hand, then showed me how his dress was "broken," and begged his new father-and-mother to give him a new one.

They are creatures of a different race. You treat them as you would treat affectionate dogs. You beat them if they pick your pockets, as they do every chance they get, and then they offer to show you the boy who did it. I never got to the point of personally beating mine, but Imam beat a few of them every day. On one occasion my donkey-boy, Hassan, was angry with me because I would not let him buy feed for the donkey, Ammon Ra, and refused to bring him up when I wanted to mount. I called to the dragoman, and said:

"Imam, Hassan won't bring up my donkey."

Imam looked at him a moment in silence, then with a lightning slap on the cheek he laid him flat in the sand. I was horrified. But to my amazement Hassan hopped up and began to kiss my sleeve and to apologize, saying, "Very good lady. Bad donkey-boy. Hassan sorry. Very good lady."

We have had three Christmases this year. The first was in Berlin, the second in Russia, and the third on the Nile—the day after the fast of Ramazan is ended. Ramazan lasts only thirty days instead of forty, like our Lent. The thirty-first is a holiday. They present each other with gifts, do no work, and picnic in the graveyards.

Between Esneh and Luxor we passed a steamer with some English officers on board, and their steamer was towing two flat-boats containing their regiments, all going to Kitchener in the Soudan. I used the field-glass on them, while my companion photographed them. We waved to them, and they waved to us and swung their hats and saluted. At Edfou they caught up with us, and passed so close to our boat that the gentlemen talked to them and asked what their regiments were. They said the Twenty-first Lancers and the Seaforth and Cameron Highlanders. Then their boat was gone. How could we know that those gallant officers of the Twenty-first Lancers would so soon lead that daring cavalry charge at Omdurman, and possibly one of those who saluted so gayly was the one killed on the awful day? It touched us very much, however, to think that they might be going to their death, and we were glad they did not belong to us, little dreaming that the blowing-up of the *Maine*, of which we had just heard, would so soon plunge our own dear country into war, and that our own fathers and brothers and friends would be marching and sailing away to defend that same "Old Glory" whose stars and stripes were floating over our heads, and whose gallant colors would succor the oppressed and avenge insult with equal promptness and equal dignity.

The temple of Denderah is not, to my mind, more beautiful than those of Luxor and Karnak; in fact, both of those are more majestic, but the mural decorations of Denderah are in a state of marvellous preservation. I own, after seeing that in some places even the original colors remained, that I quite held my breath as we approached the famous figure of Cleopatra. The sorceress of the Nile! The favorite of the goddess Hathor herself! The siren who could tempt an emperor to forsake his empire or a general to renounce fame and honor more easily than a modern woman could persuade a man to break an engagement to dine with her rival! Queen of the Lotus! Empress of the Pyramids! What grace, what charm I anticipated! I wondered if she would be portrayed floating down to meet Antony, with her purple and perfumed sails, her cloth of gold garments, her peacocks, her ibex, her lotus-blooms, and if all her mysterious fascinations would be spread before the delighted gaze of her humble worshipper.

What I found is shown in the frontispiece to this volume. Beauty unadorned with a vengeance! From this time on I shall question the taste of Antony. I only wish he could have lived to see some American girls I know.

We saw Karnak and Philae by moonlight, and we lunched in the tombs of the kings, with hieroglyphics thousands of years old looking down upon our pickled onions and cold fowl, and we ploughed through the sands at Assouan and saw the naked Nubians, with a silver ear-ring in the top of their left ear, shoot the rapids of the first cataract. We stood, too, in the temple of Luxor, before the altar of Hathor, with the sunset on one side and the moonrise on the other, and heard what her votaries say to the Goddess of Beauty. It was so mystical that we almost joined in the worship of the Egyptian Venus Aphrodite. It was so still, so majestic, so aloof from everything modern and new.

The Nile is essentially a river of silence and mystery. The ibis is always to be seen, standing alone, seemingly absorbed in meditation. The camels turn their beautiful soft eyes upon you as if you were intruding upon their silence and reserve. Never were the eyes in a human head so beautiful as a camel's. There is a limpid softness, an appealing plaintiveness in their expression which drags at your sympathies like the look in the eyes of a hunchback. It means that, with your opportunities, you might have done more with your life. Your mother looks at you that way sometimes in church, when the sermon touches a particularly raw nerve in your spiritual make-up. I always feel like apologizing when a camel looks at me.

One moonlight night was so bright that our boat started about three o'clock instead of waiting for daylight, and the start swung my state-room door open. It was so warm that I let it remain, and lay there hearing the gentle swish of the water curling against the side of the steamer, and seeing the soft moonlight form a silver pathway from the yellow bank across the river to my cabin door. The machinery made no noise. There was no more vibration than on a sail-boat. And there was the whole panorama of the Nile spread before my eyes, with all its romance and all its mystery bathed in an enchanting radiance. Occasionally a raven croaked. Sometimes a jackal howled. An obelisk made an exclamation-point against the sky, or the ruins of a temple fretted the horizon. It was the land of Ptolemy, of Rameses, of Hathor, of Horus, of Isis and Osiris, of Herodotus and Cleopatra, of Pharaoh's daughter and Moses. It was the silence of the ages which fell upon me, and then and there, in that hour of absolute stillness and solitude and beauty unspeakable, all my dreams of the Nile came true.

XII

GREECE

After our ship left Smyrna, where the camels are the finest in the world, and where the rugs set you crazy, we came across to the Piraeus, and arrived so late that very few of the passengers dared to land for fear the ship would sail without them. It was blowing a perfect gale, the sea was rough, and the captain too cross to tell us how long we would have on shore. I looked at my companion and she looked at me. In that one glance we decided that we would see the Acropolis or die in the attempt. A Cook's guide was watching our indecision with hungry eyes. We have since named him Barabbas, for reasons known to every unfortunate who ever fell into his hands. But he was clever. He said that we might cut his head off if he did not get us back to the boat in time. We assured him that we would gladly avail ourselves of his permission if that ship sailed without us. Then we scuttled down the heaving stairway at the ship's side, and away we went over (or mostly through) the waves to the Piraeus. There we took a carriage, and at the maddest gallop it ever was my lot to travel we raced up that lovely smooth avenue, between rows of wild pepper-trees which met overhead, to Athens; through Athens at a run, and reached the Acropolis, blown almost to pieces ourselves, and with the horses in a white foam.

Up to that time the Acropolis had been but a name to me. I landed because it was a sight to see, and I thought an hour or so would be better than to miss it altogether. But when I climbed that hill and set my foot within that majestic ruin, something awful clutched at my heart. I could not get my breath. The tears came into my eyes, and all at once I was helpless in the grasp of the most powerful emotion which ever has come over me in all Europe. I could not understand it, for I came in an idle mood, no more interested in it than in scores of other wonders I was thirsting to see; Luxor, Karnak, Philae, Denderah—all of those invited me quite as much as the Acropolis, but here I was speechless with surprise at my own emotion, I can imagine that such violence of feeding might turn a child into a woman, a boy into a man. All at once I saw the whole of Greek art in its proper setting. The Venus of Milo was no longer in the Louvre against its red background, where French taste has placed it, the better to set it off. Its cold, proud beauty was here again in Greece; the Hermes at Olympia; the Wingless Victory from the temple of Nike Apteros, made wingless that victory might never depart from Athens; the lovelier Winged Victory from the Louvre, with her electric poise, the most exhilarating, the most inspiring, the most intoxicating Victory the world has ever known, was loosed from her marble prison, and was again breathing the pure air of her native hills. Their white figures came crowding into my mind.

The learning of the philosophers of Greece; the "plain living and high thinking" they taught; the unspeakable purity of her art; the ineffable manner in which her masters reproduced the idea of the stern, cold pride of aloofness in these sublime types of perfect men, wrung my heart with a sense of personal loss. I can imagine that Pygmalion felt about Galatea as I felt that first hour in the Acropolis. I can imagine that a woman who had loved with the passion of her life a man of matchless integrity, of superb pride, of lofty ideals, and who had lost that love irretrievably through a fault of her own, whose gravity she first saw through his eyes when it was too late, might have felt as I felt in that hour. All the agony of a hopeless love for an art which never can return; all the sense of personal loss for the purity which I was completely realizing for the first time when it was too late; all the intense longing to have the dead past live again, that I might prove myself more worthy of it, assailed me with as mighty a force as ever the human heart could experience and still continue to beat. The piteous fragments of this lost art which remained—a few columns, the remnants of an immortal frieze, the long lines of drapery from which the head and figure were gone, the cold brow of the Hermes, the purity of his profile, the proud curve of his lips, the ineffable wanness of his smile—I could have cast myself at the foot of the Parthenon and wept over the personal disaster which befell me in that hour of realization.

I never again wish to go through such an agony of emotion. The Acropolis made the whole of Europe seem tawdry. I felt ashamed of the gorgeous sights I had seen, of the rich dinners I had eaten, of the luxuries I had enjoyed. I felt as if I would like to have the whole of my past life fall away from me as a cast-off garment, and that if I could only begin over I could do so much better with my life. I could have knelt and beat my hands together in a wild, impotent prayer for the past to be given into my keeping for just one more trial, one more opportunity to live up to the beauty and holiness and purity I had missed. When I looked up and saw the naked columns of the Parthenon silhouetted against the sky, bereft of their capitals, ragged, scarred, battered with the war of wind and weather and countless ages, all about me the ruins seemed to say, "Your appreciation is in vain; it is too late, too late!"

I have an indistinct recollection of stumbling into the

carriage, of driving down a steep road, of having the Pentelikon pointed out to me, of knowing that near that mountain lay Marathon, of seeing the statue of "Greece crowning Byron," but I heard with unhearing ears, I saw with unseeing eyes. I had left my heart and all my senses in the Acropolis. I believe that one who had left her loved one in the churchyard, on the way home for the first time to her empty house, has felt that dazed, unrealizing yet dumb heartache that I felt for days after leaving the Parthenon.

It grew worse the farther I went away from it, and for two months I have longed for Athens, Marathon, Thermopylae, Salamis. I wanted to stand and feast my soul upon the glories which were such living memories, All through Egypt and up the Nile my one wish was to live long enough and for the weeks to fly fast enough for me to get back to Athens. Now I am here for the second time, and for as long as I wish to remain.

We came sailing into the harbor just at sunset. Such a sunset! Such blue in the Mediterranean! Such a soft haze on the purple hills! How the gods must have loved Athens to place her in the garden spot of all the earth; to pour into her lap such treasures of art, and to endow her masters with power to create such an art! The approach is so beautiful. Our big black Russian ship cut her way in utter silence through the bluest of blue seas, with scarcely a ripple on the sunlit waters, between amethyst islands studded with emerald fields, making straight for that which was at one time the bravest, noblest, most courageous, most beautiful country on earth.

"The isles of Greece, the isles of Greece!
Where burning Sappho loved and sung,
Where grew the arts of war and peace,
Where Delos rose and Phoebus sprung!

Eternal summer gilds them yet,
But all except their sun is set."

Byron's statue stands in the square, surrounded by ever-greens; his picture is in the Ecole Polytechnique, and his memory and his songs are revered throughout all Greece. How her beauty tore at his soul! How her love for freedom met with an echo in his own heart! No wonder he sang, with such a theme! It was enough to give a stone song and the very rocks utterance.

It was Sunday, and as we drove through the clean, white streets, feeling absolutely hushed with the beauty which assailed us on every side, suddenly we heard the sound of music, mournful as a dirge—a martial dirge. And presently we saw approaching us the saddest, most touching yet awful procession I ever beheld. It was a military funeral. First came the band; then came two men bearing aloft the cover to the casket, wreathed in flowers and streaming with crape. Then, borne in an open coffin by four young officers of his staff, with bands of crape on their arms and knots of crape on their swords, was the dead officer, an old, gray-haired general, dressed in the full uniform of the Greek army, with his browned, wrinkled, deep-lined hands crossed over his sword. The casket was shallow, and thus he was exposed to the view of the gaping multitude, without even a glass lid to cover his bronzed face, and with the glaring sun beating down upon his closed eyes and noble gray head. Just behind him they led his riderless black horse, with his master's boots reversed in the stirrups and the empty saddle knotted with crape. It was at once majestic, heartrending, and terrible. It unnerved me, and yet it was not surprising to have such a moving spectacle greet me on my return to Greece.

We drove over the same road from the Piraeus to Athens, but in the two months of our absence they had mended a worn place in this road and had unearthed a most beautiful sarcophagus, which they placed in the national museum. The cement which held it on its pedestal was not yet dry when we saw it. They do not know its date, nor the hand of the sculptor who carved it, yet it needs no name to proclaim its beauty.

I have now seen Athens as I wanted to see it. I have seen it consecutively. It was beautiful to begin with the Acropolis and to take all day to examine just the frieze of the Parthenon. We had to have written permission, which we received through the American minister, to allow us to climb up on the scaffolding and get a near view of it. But we did it, and we were close enough to touch it, to lay our hands on it, and we waited hours for the sun to sink low enough to creep between the giant beams and touch the metopes so that we could photograph them. Of course, we could have bought photographs of them, but it seemed more like possessing them to take them with our own little cameras.

The central metope is the most beautiful and in the best state of preservation of all this marvel from the hand of Phidias; yet the work of destruction goes on, as only last year the head of the rider fell and broke into a thousand pieces, so that only the horse, the figure, and the electric splendor of his wind-blown garments floating out behind him remain. There is so little of this frieze left that it requires the full scope of the imagination, as one stands and looks at it, to picture this triumphal procession of Pan-Athenians which every four years formed at the Acropolis and wound majestically down through the Sacred Way to the Temple of Mysteries to sacrifice to the goddess in honor of Marathon and Salamis.

But we followed this road ourselves. We, too, took the Sacred Way. On the loveliest day imaginable we drove along this smooth white road; we saw the Bay of Salamis; we wound around the sweetheart curve of her shore; the purple hills forming the cup which holds her translucent waters are the background to this famous battle-ground; and beyond, set on the brow of one of these hills like a diadem, is all that remains of the Temple of Mysteries. Broken columns are there, pedestals, fragments of proud arches, now shattered and trodden under foot. Its majesty is that of a sleeping goddess, so still, so tranquil, proud even, in its ruins; yet in such utter silence it lies. In the cracks of the marble floors, in the crannies of the walls, springing from beneath the broken statue, voiceless yet persistent, grow scarlet poppies—the sleep flowers of the world, yielding to this yellowing Temple of Mysteries the quieting influence of their presence.

The next day, almost in the spirit of worship, we went to Marathon. If Salamis was my Holy Grail, then Marathon was my Mecca. We started out quite early in the morning, with relays of horses to meet us on the way. It tried to rain once or twice, but it seemed not to have the heart to spoil my crusade, for presently the sun struggled through the ragged clouds and shed a hazy half light through their edges, which completely destroyed the terrible, blinding glare and made the day simply perfect.

The road to Marathon led through orchards of cherry-trees white with blossoms, through green vineyards, past groves of olive-trees which look old enough to have seen the Persian hosts, through groups of cypress-trees, such noble sentinels of deathless evergreen; through fields of wild-cabbage blooms, making the air as sweet as the alfalfa-fields of the West; across the Valanaris by a little bridge, and suddenly an isolated farmhouse with a wine-press, and then—Marathon!

"The mountains look on Marathon,
And Marathon looks on the sea,
And musing there an hour alone,

I dreamed that Greece might still be free;
For standing by the Persian's grave,
I could not deem myself a slave!"

Marathon is only a vast plain, but what a plain! It has only a small mound in the centre to break its smoothness, but what courage, what patriotism, what nobility that mound covers! It was there, many authorities say, that all the Athenians were buried who fell at Marathon, although Byron claims that it covers the Persian dead.

How Greece has always loved freedom! In the Ecole Polytechnique are three Turkish battle-flags and some shells and cannon-balls from a war so recent that the flags have scarcely had time to dry or the shells to cool. What a pity, what an unspeakable pity, that all the glory of Greece lies in the past, and that the time of her power has gone forever! Nothing but her brave, undaunted spirit remains, and never can she live again the glories of her Salamis, her Marathon, her Thermopylae.

We have seen Athens in all her guises, the Acropolis in all her moods, at sunrise, in a thunder-storm, in the glare of mid-day, at sunset, and yet we saved the best for the climax. On the last night we were in Athens we saw the Acropolis by moonlight. We nearly upset the whole Greek government to accomplish this, for the King has issued an edict that only one night in the month may visitors be admitted, and that is the night of the full moon. But I had returned to Athens with this one idea in my mind, and if I had been obliged to go to the King myself I would have done so, and I know that I would have come away victorious. He never could have had the heart to refuse me.

It is impossible. I utterly abandon the idea of making even my nearest and dearest see what I saw and hear what I heard and think what I thought on that matchless night. There was just a breath of wind. The mountains and hills rose all around us, Lykabettos, Kolonos—the home of Sophocles—Hymettos, and Pentelikon with its marble quarries, made an undulating line of gray against the horizon, while away at the left was the Hill of Mars. How still it was! How wonderful! The rows of lights from the city converged towards the foot of the Acropolis like the topaz rays in a queen's diadem. The blue waters of the harbor glittered in the pale light. A chime of bells rang out the hour, coming faintly up to us like an echo. And above us, bathed, shrouded, swimming in silver light, was the Parthenon. The only flowers that grow at the foot of the Parthenon are the marguerites, the white-petaled, golden-hearted daisies, and even in the moonlight these starry flowers bend their tender gaze upon their god.

I leaned against one of the caryatides of the Erechtheion and looked beyond the Parthenon to the Hill of Mars, where Paul preached to the Athenians, and I believe that he must have seen the Acropolis by moonlight when he wrote, "Wherefore, when we could no longer forbear, we thought it good to be left in Athens *alone*!"

What a week we have had in Athens! If I were obliged to go home to-morrow, if Greece ended Europe for me, I could go home satisfied, filled too full of bliss to complain or even to tell what I felt. I have lived out the fullest enjoyment of my soul; I have reached the limit of my heart's desire. Athens is the goddess of my idolatry. I have turned pagan and worshipped.

In all my travels I have divided individual trips into two classes—those which would make ideal wedding journeys and those which would not. But the greatest difficulty I have encountered is how to get my happy wedded pair over here in order to *begin*. I have not the heart to ask them to risk their happiness by crossing the ocean, for the Atlantic, even by the best of ships, is ground for divorce (if you go deep enough) in itself. I have not yet tried the Pacific, but I am told that, like most people who are named Theodosia and Constance and Winifred, the Pacific does not live up to its name. However, if I could transport my people, chloroformed and by rapid transit, to Greece, I would beg of them to journey from Athens to Patras by rail; and if that exquisite experience did not smooth away all trifling difficulties and make each wish to be the one to apologize first, then I would mark them as doomed from the beginning, by their own insensate and unappreciative natures, as destined to finish their honeymoon by separate maintenance and alimony.

How I hate descriptions of scenery! How murderous I feel when the conventional novelist interrupts the most impassioned love-scene to tell how the moonlight filtered through the ragged clouds, or how the wind sighed through the naked branches of the trees, just as if anybody cared what nature was doing when human nature held the stage! And yet so marvellous is the fascination of Greece, so captivating the scenes which meet the eye from the uninviting window of a plain little foreign railroad train, that I cannot forbear to risk similar maledictions by saying that it is too heavenly for common words to express.

Now, I abominate railroads and I loathe ships. The only things I really enjoy are a rocking-chair and a book. But much as I detest the smell of car-smoke, and to find my face spotted with soot, and ill as it makes me to ride backward, I would willingly travel every month of the year over the road from Athens to Patras. The mountains are not so high as to startle, the gulf not so vast as to shock. But with gentleness you are drawn more and more into the net of its fascination until the tears well to your eyes and there is a positive physical ache in your heart.

Greece is considerate. I have seen landscapes so continuously and overpoweringly beautiful that they bored me. I know how to sympatize with Alfred Vargrave when he says to the Duc de Luvois:

"Nature is here too pretentious; her mien
Is too haughty. One likes to be coaxed, not compelled,
To the notice such beauty resents if withheld.
She seems to be saying too plainly, 'Admire me;'
And I answer, 'Yes, madam, I do; but you tire me.'"

Not so with Greece, for when you become almost intoxicated with her wonderful blues and greens and purples, and you move your head restlessly and beg a breathing-space, she compassionately recognizes your mood and lowers a silver veil over her brilliant beauty, so that you see her through a gauzy mist, which presently tantalizes you into blinking your tired eyes and wondering what she is so deftly concealing. It is like the feeling which assails you when you see a veiled statue. You long for the sculptor to chisel away the marble gauze and reveal the features. And when the craving becomes intolerable, lo! Greece, the past mistress of the art of beauty, grants your desire, and with the regal gift of a goddess brings your soul into its fruition. Cleopatra would have tantalized and left your heart to eat itself out in hopeless longing. But Cleopatra was only a queen; Venus was a goddess.

Names which were but names to you before become living realities now. We are crossing the Attic plain, and from that we find ourselves in the Thracian plain. What girl has not heard her brother spout concerning these names, famous in Greek history? Then we are in Megara, on the lovely blue Bay of Salamis. From Megara the Bay of Salamis becomes Saronic Gulf, and after an hour or two of its unspeakable beauty we cross over to Corinth and find, if possible, that the blues of the Gulf of Corinth are even more sapphire, that its purples are even more amethyst, that its greens are more emerald than the blues and purples and greens of Salamis.

From Corinth the road skirts the sea, and all these white plains are devoted to the drying of currants. At Sikyon, called "cucumber town," but originally, with the mystic beauty of the ancient Greeks, called "poppy town," the American school at Athens has made some wonderful excavations. It has discovered the supports of the stage of the famous theatre there. Then, still with the sea before us, we are at Aegium, a name full of memories of ancient Greece. It has olive, currant, grape, and mulberry plantations, and lies shrouded and bedded in beauty and romance. There, over a high iron bridge, we cross a rushing mountain torrent and are at Patras, in the moonlight, with our big ship waiting to take us across the Adriatic Sea to Brindisi.

It was with real pain that we left Greece. I would like to go back to-morrow. But there were reasons for reaching Italy without further delay, and we hurried through Corfu with only a day there to see its loveliness, instead of a week, as we would have liked. The Empress of Austria's villa lies tucked up on a hill-side, in a mass of orange, lemon, cypress, and magnolia trees. Such an enchanting picture as it presents, and such wonderful beauty as it encloses. But all that is modern. What fascinates me in Corfu is that opposite the entrance to the old Hyllaean harbor lies the isle of Pontikonisi (Mouse Island), with a small chapel and clergy-house. Tradition says that it is the Phaeacian ship which brought Ulysses to Ithaka, and which was afterwards turned into stone by the angry Poseidon (Neptune). The brook Kressida at the point where it enters the lake is also pointed out as the spot where Ulysses was cast ashore and met the Princess Nausicaa. A seasick sort of name, that!

I feel an inexplicable delight in letting my imagination run riot in the Greek traditions of their gods and goddesses. Their heroes are more real to me than Caesar and Xerxes and Alexander. And Hermes and Venus and the dwellers of Olympus have been such intimate friends since my childhood that the scenes of their exploits are of much more moment to me than Waterloo and Austerlitz. I cannot forbear laughing at myself, however, for my holy rage over Greek mythology, as founded upon no better ground than that upon which Mark Twain apologized for his admiration for Fenimore Cooper's Indians, for he admitted that they were a defunct race of beings which never had existed!

We arrived at Brindisi at four o'clock in the morning. Brindisi at four o'clock in the morning is not pleasant, nor would any other city be on the face of this green footstool. We were in quarantine, and we had to cope with a cross stewardess, who declared that we demanded too much service, and that she would *not* bring us our coffee in bed, and who then went and did it like an angel, so that we patted her on the back and told her in French that she was "well amiable," although at that hour in the morning we would have preferred to throttle her for her impertinence, and then to throw her in the Adriatic Sea as a neat little finish. Such, however, is our diplomatic course of travel.

We walked in line under the doctor's eye, and he pronounced us sanitary and permitted us to land. We were four hours late, but we scalded ourselves with a second cup of coffee and tried for the six-o'clock train for Naples, missed it, sent a telegram to Cook to send our letters to the train to meet us, and then went back to the ship to endure with patience and commendable fortitude the jeers of our fellow-passengers. Virtue was its own reward, however, for soon, under the rays of the rising sun, which we did not get up to see, and did not want to see, there steamed into the harbor alongside of us the

P. & O. ship *Sutly*, six hours ahead of time (did you ever hear of such a thing?), bearing our belated friends, the Jimmies, from Alexandria. They had been booked for the *China*, which was wrecked, so the *Sutly* took her passengers. The Jimmies had bought their passage for Venice, but we teased them to throw it up and come with us, and such is our fascination that they yielded. The love which reaches the purse is love indeed. So in a fever of joy we all caught the nine-o'clock train for Naples.

They have a sweet little way on Italian railroads of making no provision for you to eat. We did not know this, and our knowledge of Italian was limited to *Quanto tempo?* (How much time?) and *Quanto costa?* (How much is it?) So we punctuated the lovely journey among the Italian hills, and between their admirable waterways, by hopping off the train for coffee every time they said "Cinque minuti." It was like a picnic train. Half the passengers were from the P. & O., and knew the Jimmies, and the other half were from our Austrian Lloyd, and knew us, so it was perfectly delicious to see every compartment door fly open and everybody's friend appear with tea-kettles for hot water in one hand and tea-caddies in the other, and to see people who hated boiled eggs buying them, because they were about all that looked clean; and to see staid Englishmen in knickerbockers and monocles with loops of Italian bread over each tweed arm, and in both hands flasks of cheap red Italian wine—oh, so good! and only costing fifty centimes, but put up in those lovely straw-woven decanters which cost us a real pang to fling out of the window after they were emptied. And it was anything but conventional to hear one friend shout to another, "Don't pay a lira for those mandarins; I got twice that many from this pirate!" And then the five minutes would be up, and the guard would come along and call "Pronto," which is much prettier than "All aboard," but which means about the same thing; and then two ear-splitting whistles and a jangling of bells, and the doors would slam, and we were off again.

It was moonlight when we skirted the Bay of Naples—the same moonlight which lighted the Acropolis for us at Athens, which shed its silver loveliness upon the Adriatic Sea, where we had no one whose soul shared its beauty with us, and which we found again glittering upon the Bay of Naples. We stood at the car-window and watched it for an hour, for all that time our train was winding its way around the shore into Naples.

That curve of the shore, that sheet of rippling sapphire, the glint of the moon on the water, the train trailing its slow length around the bay, are associated in my mind with one of those emotional upheavals which travellers must often experience in passing from one phase of civilization to another. It marks one of the mile-stones in my inner life. I was leaving the East, the pagan East, with its mysterious influence, and I was getting back to Cooks' tourists and Italy. My mind was in a whirl. Which was best? Why should I so love one, and why did the other bore me? I was afraid to follow the yearnings of my own soul, and yet I knew that only there lay happiness. To make up one's mind to be true to one's love—even if it be only the love of beauty—requires courage. And the trial of my bravery came to me on that curve of the Bay of Naples. I dared. I am daring now. I am still true to the Orient.

As I look back I remember that the phrase, "See Naples and die," gave me the hazy idea that it must be very beautiful, but just how I did not know, and did not particularly care. I knew the bay would be lovely; I only hoped it would be as lovely as I expected. Celebrated beauties are so apt to be disappointing. I imagined that all Neapolitan boys wore their shirt-collars open and that a wavy lock of coal-black hair was continually blowing across their brown foreheads. That eternal porcelain miniature has maddened me with its omnipresence ever since I was a child. But aside from these half-thoughts and dim expectations I had no hopes at all. I was prepared to be gently and tranquilly pleased; not wildly excited, but satisfied; not happy, but contented with its beauty. But I have found more. The bay is more lovely than I anticipated, and I have discovered that Italian hair is not coal-black; it begins to be black at the roots, and evidently had every intention of being black when it started out, but it grew weary of so much energy, and ended in sundry shades of russet brown and sunburned tans. It generally has these two colors, black and tan, like the silky coat of a fine terrier, and it waves in lovely little tendrils, and is much prettier than hair either all black or all brown.

But I am ahead of my narrative. I am trying to decide whether Naples is more beautifully situated than Constantinople. Constantinople, being Oriental, fascinates me more. Western Europe begins to seem a little tame and conventional to me, because the pagan in my nature is so highly developed. I detest civilization except for my own selfish bodily comfort. When I eat and sleep I want the creature comforts. Otherwise I love those thieving Arab servants in Cairo (who would steal the very shoes off your feet if you dropped off for your forty winks) because of their uncivilization and unconventionality. Civilization has not yet spoiled them. I bought rugs in Cairo, and often when I went unexpectedly into my room I found my Arab man-servant on his knees studying their patterns and feeling their silkiness. I had everything locked up, or perhaps he would have made worse use of his time; but somehow the childishness of the East appeals to me.

Constantinople is so delightfully dirty and old. Mrs. Jimmie sniffs at me because I can stop the peasants who lead their cows through the streets of Naples, and because I can drink a glass of warm milk; Mrs. Jimmie wants hers strained. But if I can eat "Turkish Delight" in Constantinople, buying it in the bazaars, seeing it cut off the huge sticky mass with rusty lamp-scissors, perhaps dropped on the dirt-floor, and in a moment of abstraction polished off on the Turk's trousers and rolled in soft sugar to wrap the real in the ideal—if I can cope with *that* problem, surely a trifle like drinking unstrained milk, with the consoling satisfaction of stopping the carriage in an adorable spot, with the blue waters of the bay curling up on its shore down below on the right, and a sheer cliff covered with moss and clinging vines and surmounted by a superb villa on the left, is nothing. For to eat or to drink amid such romantic surroundings, even if it were unstrained milk, was an experience not to be despised.

Yet here are two cities situated like amphitheatres upon the convex curve of two ideally beautiful harbors. How do you compare them? Each according to your own temper and humor. You have seen hundreds of colored photographs both of Naples and Constantinople. But of the two you will find only Naples exactly like the pictures. Everybody agrees about Naples. People disagree delightfully about Constantinople. Some can never get beyond the dirt and smells and thievery. Some never get used to the delicious thrills of surprise which every turn and every corner and every vista and every night and every morning hold for the beauty-lover. Nothing could be more heterodox, more *bizarre*, more unconventional than Constantinople scenes. Nothing could be more orthodox than the views of Naples. To be sure, poets have written reams of poetry about it, travellers have sent home pages of rhapsodies about it, tourists have conscientiously "done" the town, with their heads cocked on one side and their forefingers on a paragraph in Baedeker; but just *because* of this, *because* everybody on earth who ever has been to Naples—man or woman, Jew or Gentile, black or white, bond or free—*has* wept and gurgled and had hysteria over its mild and placid beauty, is one reason why I find it somewhat tame. Italian scenery seems to me laid out by a landscape-gardener. Its beauty is absolutely conventional. Nobody will blame you if you admire it. To rave over it is like going to church—it is the proper thing to do. People will raise their eyebrows if you don't, and watch what you eat, and speculate on your ancestry, and wonder about your politics.

The beauty of Italy is so proper and Church of England that you are looked upon as a dissenter if you do not rhapsodize about it. But it disappoints me to feel obliged to follow the multitude like a flock of sheep and to take the dust of those feeble-minded tourists who have preceded me and set the pace. There is nothing in the scenery of all Italy to shock your love of beauty from the staid to the original. There is nothing to give your sensitive soul little shivers of surprise. There is nothing to make you hesitate for fear you ought not to admire; you *know* you ought. You feel obliged to do so because everybody has done it before you, and you will be thought queer if you don't. There is a gentle, pretty-pretty haze of romance over Italian scenery which is like reading fairy-tales after having devoured Carlyle. It is like hearing Verdi after Wagner. The East has my real love. I find that I cannot rave over a pink and white china shepherdess when I have worshipped the Venus of Milo.

Lilian Bell

XIII

NAPLES

The point of view is always the pivot of recollection. How ought one to remember a place? There are a dozen ways of enjoying Naples, and twenty ways of being miserable in America. Or turn it the other way, it makes no difference. It depends upon one's self and the state of the spleen. Before I came to Europe I remember often to have been disgusted with persons who recalled Germany by its beer and Spain by its fleas, or those who said: "Cologne! Oh yes; I remember we got such a good breakfast there."

Ah, ha! It is so easy to sniff when one is mooning in imagination over cathedrals, but I have since taken back all those sniffs. I did not realize then the misery of standing on one foot all the morning in tombs, and on the other all the afternoon in museums, and then of going home to sleep on an ironing-board. Now I, too, think gratefully of the Bay of Naples as being near that good bed, and of the Pyramids as being near the excellent table of Shepheard's. Why not? Can one rave over Vesuvius on an empty stomach, or get all the beauty out of Sorrento with a backache? One must be well and have good spirits when one travels. It is not so essential merely to be comfortable, although that helps wonderfully. But even to get soaking wet could not utterly spoil the road to Posilipo. What a heavenly drive! Although I think with more fondness of scaling the heights of Capri in a trembling little Italian cab, not because both views were not divinely beautiful, but because when in Capri my clothes were not damply sticking to me, and I had no puddle of water in each shoe. As I look back I believe I could write specific directions from personal experience on "How to be Happy when Miserable." Jimmie always bewails the fact that the American girl lives on her nerves. "Goes on her uppers" is his choice phrase. Nevertheless, it pulled us through many a mental bog while travelling so continuously.

Therefore, from a dozen different recollections of Naples, eleven of which you may read in your red-covered Baedeker, or *Recollections of Italy*, or *Leaves from my Note-Book*, or *Memories of Blissful Hours*, and similar productions, I have most poignantly to remember our shopping experiences in Naples. But before launching my battleship I owe an apology to the worshippers of Italy. I can appreciate their rapturous memories. I share in a measure their enthusiasm. To a certain temper Italy would be adorable for a honeymoon or to return to a second or a fifth time. But it is not in human nature, after having come from Russia, Egypt, and Greece, to have one's pristine enthusiasm to pour out in torrents over the ladylike beauty of Italy, because these other countries are so much more unfrequented, more pagan, and more fascinating. But in daring to say that, I again pull my forelock to Italy's worshippers.

To begin with, we were robbed all through Italy; not robbed in a common way, but, to the honor of the Italians let me say, robbed in a highly interesting and somewhat exciting manner.

Somebody has said, "What a beautiful country Italy would be if it were not for the Italians!" We are used to having our things stolen, and to being overcharged for everything just because we are Americans, but we are not used to the utter brigandage of Italy. On the Russian ship coming from Odessa to Constantinople some of the second-cabin passengers got into our state-rooms during dinner and went through our hand-baggage, which we had left unlocked, and stole my ulster. And, of course, in Constantinople they warned us not to trust the Greeks, for it is their form of comparison to say, "He lies like a Greek," while in Greece the worst thing they can say is that "He steals like a Turk." In Cairo it was not necessary to warn us, for everybody knows what liars and thieves Arabs are. Not a day went by on those donkey excursions on the Nile that the men did not have their pockets picked. The passengers on the *Mayflower* lost enough silk handkerchiefs to start a haberdasher's shop, and every woman lost money. In Cairo, whether you go to the bazaars or to a mosque to see the faithful at their prayers, your dragoman tells you not to have anything of value in your pockets, and not to carry your purse in your hand.

But we had not even got through the custom-house at Brindisi, when Gaze's man recommended us to have our trunks corded and sealed, for they are sometimes broken open on the train. We thought this rather a useless precaution, but Jimmie has travelled so much that he made us do it. It seems that the King has admitted that he is powerless to stop these outrages, and so he begs foreign travellers to protect themselves, inasmuch as he is unable to protect them.

We stayed at the smartest hotel in Naples, but we had not been there two days before Jimmie's valises were broken open, and all his studs and forty pounds in money were stolen. That frightened us almost to death, but something worse happened. One day at three o'clock in the afternoon my companion was sitting in her room writing a letter, and she happened to look up just in time to see the handle of the door turn slowly and softly.

Then the door opened a crack, still without a sound, and a man with a black beard put in his head. As he met her eyes fixed squarely upon him he closed the door as silently as a shadow. She hurried after him and looked out, and ran up the corridor peering into every possible corner, but no man could she see. He had disappeared as completely as if he had been a ghost. She reported it to the proprietor, but he shrugged his shoulders, and said, "Madam must have imagined it!"

By this time we were all feeling rather creepy. However, as Jimmie says when we are all tired out and hungry and cross, "Cheer up. The worst is yet to come."

One day my companion and Mrs. Jimmie and I went to one of the best shops in all Italy, to buy a ring. Mrs. Jimmie was getting it for her husband's birthday.

Now, Mrs. Jimmie's own rings are extremely beautiful, and her very handsomest consists of a band of blue-white matched diamonds which exactly fills the space between her two fingers, and is so heavy and so fine that only Tiffany could duplicate it. The band of the ring is merely a fine wire. To try on Jimmie's ring, Mrs. Jimmie took off all hers and laid them on the counter. Now, mind you, this was a famous jeweller's where this happened. But when she had decided to take the new ring, and turned to put on her own again, lo! this especial ring was gone. We searched everywhere. We told the clerk, but he said she had not worn such a ring. This was the first thing which made us suspect that something was wrong. We insisted, and he reiterated. Finally, I made up my mind. I said to my companion: "You stand at the front door and have Mrs. Jimmie stand at the side door. Don't you permit any one either to enter or leave, while I rush around to

Cook's office and find out what can be done." Both women turned pale, but obeyed me. One clerk started for the back door, but we called him and told him that no one was to move until we could get the police there. Then such a scurrying and *such* a begging as there was! Would madam wait just one moment? Would madam permit them to call the proprietor? (Anybody would have thought it was *my* ring, for Mrs. Jimmie's calm was not even ruffled, while *I* was in a white heat, and all their impassioned appeals were addressed to me!) I said they could call the proprietor if they could call him without leaving the room. They called him in Italian. He came, a little, smooth, brown man, with black, shoe-button eyes. We explained to him just what had taken place, Mrs. Jimmie with her back against one door, and my companion braced against the side door, like Ajax defying the lightning.

He rubbed his hands, and listened to a torrent of excited Italian from no fewer than ten crazy clerks. Then I stated the case in English. The proprietor turned to Mrs. Jimmie, and said if madam was so sure that she had worn a ring, which all his clerks assured him she had not worn, then, for the honor of his house, he must beg madam to choose another ring, of whatever value she liked, and it should be a present from him!

Now, Mrs. Jimmie is a very Madonna of calmness, but at that she ignited. She told him that Tiffany had been six months matching those stones, and that not in all his shop— not in the whole of Italy—could he find a duplicate. At that another search took place, and I, just to make things pleasant, started for the American ambassador's. (I had risen a peg from Cook's!) Such pleading! Such begging! Two of the clerks actually wept—Italian tears. When lo! a shout of triumph, and from a remote corner of the shop, quite forty feet from us, in a place where we had not been, under a big vase, they found that ring! If it had had the wings of a swallow it could not have flown there. If it had had the legs of a centipede it could not have crawled there. The proprietor was radiant in his unctuous satisfaction. "It had rolled there!" Rolled! That ring! It had no more chance of rolling than a loaded die! We all sniffed, and sniffed publicly. Mrs. Jimmie, I regret to say, was weak enough to buy the ring she had ordered for Jimmie in spite of this occurrence. But I think I don't blame her. I am weak myself about buying things. But *that* is a sample of Italian honesty, and in a shop which would rank with our very best in New York or Chicago. Heaven help Italy!

Italian politeness is very cheap, very thin-skinned, and, like the French, only for the surface. They pretend to trust you with their whole shop; they shower you with polite attentions; you are the Great and Only while you are buying. But I am of the opinion that you are shadowed by a whole army of spies if you owe a cent, and that for lack of plenty of suspicion and prompt action to recover I am sure that neither the Italians nor the French ever lost a sou.

We went into the best tortoise-shell shop in all Naples to buy one dozen shell hair-pins, but such was the misery we experienced at leaving any of the treasures we encountered that we bought three hundred dollars' worth before we left, and of course did not have enough money to pay for them. So we said to lay the things aside for us, and we would draw some money at our banker's, and pay for them when we came to fetch them.

Not for the world, declared this Judas Iscariot, this Benedict Arnold of an Italian Jew! We must take the things with us. Were we not Americans, and by Americans did he not live? Behold, he would take the articles with his own hands to our carriage. And he did, despite our protests. But the villain drew on us through our banker before we were out of bed the next morning! I felt like a horse-thief.

However, I confess to a weakness for the overwhelmingly polite attentions one receives from Italian and French shopkeepers. One gets none of it in Germany, and in America I am always under the deepest obligations if the haughty "sales-ladies" and "sales-gentlemen" will wait on the men and women who wish to buy. I am accustomed to the ignominy of being ignored, and to the insult of impudence if I protest; but why, oh, why, do politeness and honesty so seldom go together?

There is a decency about Puritan America which appeals to me quite as much as the rugged honesty of American shopkeepers. The unspeakable street scenes of Europe would be impossible in America. In Naples all the mysteries of the toilet are in certain quarters of the city public property, and the dressing-room of children in particular is bounded by north, east, south, and west, and roofed by the sky.

I have seen Italians comb their beards over their soup at dinner. I have seen every Frenchman his own manicure at the opera. I have seen Germans take out their false teeth at the *table d'hote* and rinse them in a glass of water, but it remains for Naples to cap the climax for Sunday-afternoon diversions.

A curious thing about European decency is that it seems to be forced on people by law, and indulged in only for show. The Gallic nations are only veneered with decency. They have, almost to a man, none of it naturally, or for its own sake. Take, for example, the sidewalks of Paris after dark. The moment public surveillance wanes or the sun goes down the Frenchman becomes his own natural self.

The Neapolitan's acceptation of dirt as a portion of his

inheritance is irresistibly comic to a pagan outsider. To drive down the Via di Porto is to see a mimic world. All the shops empty themselves into the street. They leave only room for your cab to drive through the maze of stalls, booths, chairs, beds, and benches. At nightfall they light flaring torches, which, viewed from the top of the street, make the descent look like a witch scene from an opera.

It is the street of the very poor, but one is struck by the excellent diet of these same very poor. They eat as a staple roasted artichokes—a great delicacy with us. They cook macaroni with tomatoes in huge iron kettles over charcoal fires, and sell it by the plateful to their customers, often hauling it out of the kettles with their hands, like a sailor's hornpipe, pinching off the macaroni if it lengthens too much, and blowing on their fingers to cool them. They have roasted chestnuts, fried fish, boiled eggs, and long loops of crisp Italian bread strung on a stake. There are scores of these booths in this street, the selling conducted generally by the father and grown sons, while the wife sits by knitting in the smoke and glare of the torches, screaming in peasant Italian to her neighbor across the way, commenting quite openly upon the people in the cabs, and wondering how much their hats cost. The bambinos are often hung upon pegs in the front of the house, where they look out of their little black, beady eyes like pappooses. I unhooked one of these babies once, and held it awhile. Its back and little feet were held tightly against a strip of board so that it was quite stiff from its feet to its shoulders. It did not seem to object or to be at all uncomfortable, and as it only howled while I was holding it I have an idea that, except when invaded by foreigners, the bambino's existence is quite happy. Babies seem to be no trouble in Italy, and one cannot but be struck by the number of them. One can hardly remember seeing many French babies, for the reason that there are so few to remember—so few, indeed, that the French government has put a premium upon them; but in Naples the pretty mothers with their pretty babies, playing at bo-peep with each other like charming children, are some of the most delightful scenes in this fascinating Street of the Door.

These bambinos hooked against the wall look down upon curious scenes. Their mothers bring their wash-tubs into the street, wash the clothes in plain view of everybody, hang them on clothes-lines strung between two chairs, while a diminutive charcoal-stove, with half a dozen irons leaning against its sides, stands in the doorway ready to perform its part in the little scene. I saw a boy cooking two tiny smelts over a tailor's goose. The handle was taken off, and the fish were frying so merrily over the glowing coals, and they looked so good, and the odor which steamed from them was so ravishing, that I wanted to ask him if I might not join him and help him cook two more.

In point of fact, Naples seems like a holiday town, with everybody merely playing at work, or resting from even that pretence. The Neapolitans are so essentially an out-of-door people and a leisurely people that it seems a crime to hurry. The very goats wandering aimlessly through the streets, nibbling around open doorways, add an element of imbecile helplessness to a childish people.

Did you ever examine a goat's expression of face? For utter asininity a donkey cannot approach him. Nothing can, except, perhaps, an Irish farce-comedian.

Beautiful cows are driven through the streets, often attended by the owner's family. The mother milks for the passing customers, the father fetches it all lovely and foaming and warm to your cab, and the pretty, big-eyed children caper around you, begging for a "macaroni" instead of a "pourboire."

Then, instead of dining at your smart hotel, it is so much more adorable to drop in at some charming restaurant with tables set in the open air, and to hear the band play, and to eat all sorts of delicious unknowable dishes, and to drink a beautiful golden wine called "Lachrima Christi" (the tears of Christ), and to watch the people—the people—the people!

XIV

ROME

On Easter Sunday I had my first view of Rome, my first view of St. Peter's. The day was as soft and mild as one of our own spring days, and there was even that little sharp tang in the air which one feels in the early spring in America. The wind was sweet and balmy, yet now and then it had a sharp edge to it as it cut around a curve, as if to remind one that the frost was not yet all out of the ground, and that the sun was still only the heir-apparent to the throne and had not yet been crowned king. It was the sort of day that one has at home a little later, when one still likes the feel of the fur around the neck, while the trees are still bare, when the eager spring wind brings a tingle to the blood and the smell of rich, black earth and early green springing things to the nostrils; when the eye is ravished with the sight of purple hyacinths thrusting their royal chalices up through the reluctant soil; when the sun-colored jonquil and the star-eyed narcissus lift their scented heads above the sombre ground, as if uncon- scious of the patches of snow here and there, forming one of the contradictions of life, but a contradiction always welcome, because it is in itself a promise of better things to come.

Not in the full fruition of a rose-laden June or in the golden days of Indian summer or the ruddy autumn or the white holiness of Christmas-tide—not in the beauties of the whole year is there anything so exhilarating, so thrilling, so intoxicating as these first days of spring, which always come with a delicious shock of surprise, before one suspects their approach or has time to grow weary with waiting. Nothing, nothing in the world smells like a spring wind! It is full of youth and promise and inspiration. One forgets all the falseness of its promises last year, all the disappointment of the past summer, and, charged with its bewildering electricity, one builds a thousand air-castles as to what *this* year will bring forth, based on no surer a foundation than the smell of melting snow and fresh black earth and yellow and purple spring flowers which are blown across one's ever-hopeful soul by a breath of eager, tingling spring wind.

I shall never forget that first drive in Rome on such a day as this, which brought my own beloved country so forcibly to my mind. There were rumors of war in the air, and my heart was heavy for my country, but I forgot all my forebodings as we drew up before the majestic steps of St. Peter's, for I felt that something would happen to avert disaster from our shores and keep my country safe and victorious.

St. Peter's had a curious effect upon me. It was too big and too secular and too boastful for a church, too poor in art treasures for a successful museum, the music too inadequate to suit me with the echoes of the Tzar's choir still ringing in my ears, and the lack of pomp compared to the Greek churches left me with a longing to hunt up more gold lace and purple velvet. There was nothing like the devoutness of the Russians in the worshippers I saw in Rome. I stood a long time by the statue of the Pope. His toe was nearly kissed off, but every one carefully wiped off the last kiss before placing his or her own, thereby convincing me of the universal belief in the microbe theory. The whole attitude of the Roman mind is different. Here it is a religious duty. In Russia it is a sacrament.

There were thousands of people in St. Peter's, many of whom—the best-dressed and the worst-behaved—were Americans. It seemed very homelike and intimate to hear my own language spoken again, even if it were sometimes sadly mutilated. But I remember St. Peter's that Easter Sunday chiefly because I had with me a sympathetic companion; one who knew that St. Peter's was not a place to talk; one who knew enough to absorb in silence; one, in fact, who understood! Such comprehensive silence was to my ragged spirit balm and healing.

Beware, oh, beware with whom you travel! One uncongenial person in the party—one man who sneers at sentiment, one woman whose point of view is material—can ruin the loveliest journey and dampen one's heavenliest enthusiasm.

In order to travel properly, one ought to be in vein. It is as bad to begin a journey with a companion who gets on one's nerves as it is to sit down to a banquet and quarrel through the courses. The effect is the same. One can digest neither. People seem to select travelling companions as recklessly as they marry. They generally manage to start with the wrong one. I often shudder to hear two women at a luncheon say, "Why not arrange to go to Europe together next year?" And yet I solace myself with the thought, "Why not? If you considered! your list of friends for a month, and selected the most desirable, you would probably make even a worse mistake, for travelling develops hatred more than any other one thing I know of; so, in addition to spoiling your journey, you would also lose your friend—or wish you *could* lose her!"

George Eliot has said that there was no greater strain on

friendship than a dissimilarity of taste in jests. But I am inclined to believe George Eliot never travelled extensively, else, without disturbing that statement, she would have added, "or a dissimilarity in point of view with one's travelling companion."

It makes no difference which one's view is the loftier. It is the dissimilarity which rasps and grates. Doubtless the material is as much irritated by the spiritual as the poetic is fretted by the prosaic. It is worse than to be at a Wagner matinee with a woman who cares only for Verdi. One wishes to nudge her arm and feel a sympathetic pressure which means, "Yes, yes, so do I!" It is awful not to be able to nudge! Speech is seldom imperative, but understanding signals is as necessary to one's soul-happiness as air to the lungs. So Greece with one who has but a Baedeker knowledge of art, or Rome to one who remembers her history vaguely as something that she "took" at school, is simply maddening to one who forgets the technicalities of dates and formulas, and rapturously breathes it in, scarcely knowing whence came the love or knowledge of it, but realizing that one has at last come into one's kingdom.

I was singularly fortunate from time to time in discovering these kindred, sympathetic spirits. I met one party of three in Egypt, and found them again in Greece, and crossed to Italy with them. It was a mother and son and a lovely girl. They will never know, unless they happen across this page, how much they were to me on the Adriatic, and what a void they filled in Athens.

I found another such at Capri and Pompeii, and those beautiful days stand out in my mind more for the company I was in than even the wonders we went to see. That statement is strong but true. Yet my various other fellow-travellers who were lacking in the one essential of soul would never believe it, inasmuch as a person without a soul cannot miss what she never had, and will not believe what she cannot comprehend. I met one ill-assorted couple of that kind once. They were two young women—sisters. One had imagination, soul, fire, poetry, and all that goes to make up genius; but lacking as she did executive ability and perseverance, her genius was inarticulate. The impersonal world would never know her beauties, but her friends were rich in her acquaintance. Her sister was a walking Baedeker—red cover, gold letters, and all. She was "doing Europe." She read her guide-book, she saw nothing beyond, and the only time that she really blossomed was when dressing for *table d'hote* dinners. I found them at the Grand Hotel at Rome—one of the most beautiful and well-kept hotels, and one admirably adapted to display the tourist who tours on principle.

This gorgeous hotel on Easter week is a sight for gods and men. We engaged our rooms here while we were on the Nile, two months before, and reminded them once a week all during that time that we were coming; otherwise, on account of its extreme popularity in the fashionable world, they might not have been able to hold them for us. We reached there late on the Saturday evening before Easter, and dined in our own apartments. But the next day, and indeed until war broke out and we fled from Rome, the Grand Hotel was as delightful as it was possible to make a gorgeous, luxurious, and fashionable hotel. The palm-room, where the band plays for afternoon tea, and where one always comes for one's coffee, is between the entrance and the grand dining-room, so that on entering the hotel one comes upon a most beautiful vista of a series of huge glass doors and lovely green waving palms, with nothing but a glass roof between one and the blue Italian sky.

Most of the smart Americans go there, and a very beautiful front they presented. I had not seen any American clothes for a year, but on Easter Sunday at luncheon I saw the most bewitching array of smart street-gowns worn by the inimitable American woman, who is as far beyond the women of every other race on earth in her selection of clothes and the way she holds up her head and her shoulders back and walks off in them as grand opera is above a hand-organ. Even the French woman does not combine the good sense with good taste as the American does. And there I found these sisters, each lovely in her own way—the pretty one listening to the raptures of the poetic one with a palpable sneer which said plainly: "I not only have no part in these vain imaginings, but I do not think that you yourself believe them. You are posing for the world, and I am the only one who knows it. Have I not been with you everywhere, and have I, with my two eyes, which certainly are as good as yours—have I seen these things you describe?" It was pathetic, for the muse of the poet soon felt the mire in which it daily trod. The fire faded from the girl's eye, her radiance disappeared, her noble enthusiasms paled, her fantastic and brilliant imagination dulled, and soon she sat listlessly in our midst, a tired, patient smile upon her delicate face, while her sister discoursed volubly upon clothes. Alas, the old fable of the iron pot and the porcelain kettle drifting down the stream together! At the end of the journey the iron pot had not even a scratch upon its thick sides, but the porcelain was broken to pieces. How I longed to take that wounded imagination, that whimsical wit, under my wing and explore Rome with her! But circumstances held the two together, and I took instead my guide, Seraphino Malespina. Seraphino deserves a chapter by himself. His observations upon human nature were of much more value to me than his knowledge of Rome, accurate and worthy as that was. He was the best guide I ever had. I had heard of him, so when we arrived I simply wrote to him and engaged him by the week. He took us everywhere, never wasted our money (which is a wonder in a guide), and, while I may forget some of his dates and statistics, I shall never forget his shrewdness in understanding human nature. His disquisitions on the ordinary tourist, and his acute analysis of the two sisters I have described, were so accurate that I determined then and there that Seraphino was a philosopher. The interest I took in his narratives pleased him to such an extent that he was unwearied in searching out interesting material. I taught him to use the camera, and he photographed us in the Colosseum and in front of the Arch of Constantine.

He persuaded me to coax the poet away from her sister one day and to take her with me instead of my companion. I did so, and to this day I thank my guide for his wisdom, for once out from under the sister's depressing influence, that whimsical genius, worthy of being classed with the most famous of wits, blossomed under my appreciative laughter like a rose in the sunlight.

We saw, too, the magnificent statue of Garibaldi—a superb thing, which overlooks the whole city of Rome. We tossed pennies into the fountain of the Trevi, and drank some of the water, which is a sure sign, if you wish it at the time you drink, that you will return to Rome.

It was on the day that we went to Tivoli that I heard the first war news from America which I regarded final. We were on the Nile when the *Maine* was blown up, and all through Egypt and Greece news was slow to travel. When we got to Italy we were dependent upon London for despatches. I waited until I received my own papers before I knew the truth. Finally, on our departure for Tivoli, my American mail was handed to me, and I found what preparations were being made—that my brother was going! I remember Tivoli as in a haze of war-clouds. America arming herself for war once more! Some of my family—my very own—preparing to go! How much do you think I cared for the Emperor Hadrian and his villa, which was a whole town in itself, and his waterfalls and his wonderful objects of art?

At any other time how I would have revelled in the idea of his two theatres, his schools, his libraries, his statues pillaged from my beautiful Greece, his philosopher's wall—a huge wall built only for shade, so that his friends who came to discourse philosophy with him could walk in its west shadow mornings, and in its east shadow afternoons; all these things would have driven me wild with enthusiasm. But on that day I saw instead the Flying Squadron in Hampton Roads, painted black. I saw the President and his secretaries, with anxious faces, consulting with their generals; I saw how awful must be the sacrifice to the country in every way— money, commerce, health, the very lives of the dear soldiers of *our* army, who fight from choice, and not because law compels their enlistment. My companion ridiculed my anxiety and rallied me on my inattention to Hadrian. Hadrian! What was Hadrian to me when I thought of the volunteers in America?

Not two days later war was formally declared, and although Rome was yet practically unexplored, although we had been there only three weeks, we rushed post-haste to Paris, spent one day gathering up our trunks from Munroe's, and left that same night for London.

Once in London, however, we found ourselves blocked. The American Line steamships had been requisitioned by the government, and were no longer at our disposal. With changed names they were turned into war vessels, and few, indeed, were the women who would go aboard them in the near future. The North German Lloyd promised us the new *Kaiser Friedrich*, and every place was taken. We went to the Cecil Hotel and waited. Day after day passed, and the sailing-day was postponed once, then twice. I was frantic with impatience. The truth was the *Kaiser Friedrich* was not quite finished. Evidently it is the same with a ship as with dress-makers. They promise to finish your gown and send it home for Thanksgiving, whereas you are in luck if you get it by Christmas.

The only thing that consoled me was being at the Cecil. To be sure, it was filled with Americans, but I was not avoiding them then. I had finished my journeyings. I had got my point of view. I was going HOME!

How I wished for poor Bee! What an awful time she had with me at "The Insular"! (which, of course, is not its real name; but I dare not tell it, because it is so smart, and I would shock its worshippers). How she hated our lodgings! Now she will not believe me when I tell her that the Cecil is as good as an American hotel; that its elevators (lifts) really move; that its cuisine is as delicious as Paris; that its service is excellent. Bee is polite but incredulous. To be sure, I tell her that the hotel is as ugly as *only* an English architect could make it; that the blue tiles in the dining-room would make of it a fine natatorium, if they would only shut the doors and turn in the water—nothing convinces her that English hotels are not jellied nightmares. But as for me, I recall the Cecil with feelings of the liveliest appreciation. I was comfortable there, for the first time in England. If it had not been for the war I would have been happy.

The hotels in London which the English consider the best I consider the worst. If an American wishes to be comfortable let him eschew all other gods and cleave to the Cecil. The Cecil! I wish my cab was turning in at the entrance this very minute!

Finally the *Kaiser Friedrich* burst something important in her interior, and they gave her up and put on the *Trave*.

Instantly there was a maddened rush for the Liverpool steamer. The Cunard office was besieged. Within two hours after the North German Lloyd bulletined the *Trave* every berth was taken on the *Etruria*. I arrived too late, so, in company with the most of the *Kaiser Friedrich's* passengers, I resigned myself to the *Trave*.

We were eight days at sea, and some of those I remained in my berth. I was happier there, and yet in spite of private woes I still think of that delightful captain and that darling stewardess with affection. The steamship company literally outdid themselves in their efforts to console their disappointed passengers. They put the town of Southampton at our disposal, and the *Trave's* steady and spinster-like behavior did the rest.

I held receptions in my state-room every day. The captain called every morning, and so did the charming wife of the returning German Ambassador, Mr. Uhl. The girls came down and sat on my steamer-trunk, and told me of the flirtations going on on deck. And every night that dear stewardess would come and tuck me in, and turn out the light, and say, "Good-night, fraeulein; I hope you feel to-morrow better."

When the pilot reached us we were at luncheon, and every man in the dining-room bolted. American newspapers after eight days of suspense! One man stood up and read the news aloud. Dewey and the battle of Manila Bay! We did not applaud. It was too far off and too unreal. But we women wept.

As we drove through the streets of New York I said to the people who came to meet me, "For Heaven's sake, what are all these flags out for? Is it Washington's birthday? I have lost count of time!"

Lilian Bell

My cousin looked at me pityingly.

"My poor child," she said, "I am glad you have come back to God's country, where you can learn something. We have a war on!"

I gave a gasp. That shows how unreal the war seemed to me over there. I never saw so many flags as I saw in Jersey City and New York. I was horrified to find Chicago, nay, even my own house, lacking in that respect.

But I am proud to relate that two hours after my return— directly I had done kissing Billy, in fact—the largest flag on the whole street was floating from my study window.

Choose from Thousands of 1stWorldLibrary Classics By

A. M. Barnard
Ada Leverson
Adolphus William Ward
Aesop
Agatha Christie
Alexander Aaronsohn
Alexander Kielland
Alexandre Dumas
Alfred Gatty
Alfred Ollivant
Alice Duer Miller
Alice Turner Curtis
Alice Dunbar
Allen Chapman
Alleyne Ireland
Ambrose Bierce
Amelia E. Barr
Amory H. Bradford
Andrew Lang
Andrew McFarland Davis
Andy Adams
Angela Brazil
Anna Alice Chapin
Anna Sewell
Annie Besant
Annie Hamilton Donnell
Annie Payson Call
Annie Roe Carr
Annonaymous
Anton Chekhov
Archibald Lee Fletcher
Arnold Bennett
Arthur C. Benson
Arthur Conan Doyle
Arthur M. Winfield
Arthur Ransome
Arthur Schnitzler
Arthur Train
Atticus
B.H. Baden-Powell
B. M. Bower
B. C. Chatterjee
Baroness Emmuska Orczy
Baroness Orczy
Basil King
Bayard Taylor
Ben Macomber
Bertha Muzzy Bower
Bjornstjerne Bjornson

Booth Tarkington
Boyd Cable
Bram Stoker
C. Collodi
C. E. Orr
C. M. Ingleby
Carolyn Wells
Catherine Parr Traill
Charles A. Eastman
Charles Amory Beach
Charles Dickens
Charles Dudley Warner
Charles Farrar Browne
Charles Ives
Charles Kingsley
Charles Klein
Charles Hanson Towne
Charles Lathrop Pack
Charles Romyn Dake
Charles Whibley
Charles Willing Beale
Charlotte M. Braeme
Charlotte M. Yonge
Charlotte Perkins Stetson
Clair W. Hayes
Clarence Day Jr.
Clarence E. Mulford
Clemence Housman
Confucius
Coningsby Dawson
Cornelis DeWitt Wilcox
Cyril Burleigh
D. H. Lawrence
Daniel Defoe
David Garnett
Dinah Craik
Don Carlos Janes
Donald Keyhoe
Dorothy Kilner
Dougan Clark
Douglas Fairbanks
E. Nesbit
E. P. Roe
E. Phillips Oppenheim
E. S. Brooks
Earl Barnes
Edgar Rice Burroughs
Edith Van Dyne
Edith Wharton

Edward Everett Hale
Edward J. O'Biren
Edward S. Ellis
Edwin L. Arnold
Eleanor Atkins
Eleanor Hallowell Abbott
Eliot Gregory
Elizabeth Gaskell
Elizabeth McCracken
Elizabeth Von Arnim
Ellem Key
Emerson Hough
Emilie F. Carlen
Emily Bronte
Emily Dickinson
Enid Bagnold
Enilor Macartney Lane
Erasmus W. Jones
Ernie Howard Pie
Ethel May Dell
Ethel Turner
Ethel Watts Mumford
Eugene Sue
Eugenie Foa
Eugene Wood
Eustace Hale Ball
Evelyn Everett-green
Everard Cotes
F. H. Cheley
F. J. Cross
F. Marion Crawford
Fannie E. Newberry
Federick Austin Ogg
Ferdinand Ossendowski
Fergus Hume
Florence A. Kilpatrick
Fremont B. Deering
Francis Bacon
Francis Darwin
Frances Hodgson Burnett
Frances Parkinson Keyes
Frank Gee Patchin
Frank Harris
Frank Jewett Mather
Frank L. Packard
Frank V. Webster
Frederic Stewart Isham
Frederick Trevor Hill
Frederick Winslow Taylor

Friedrich Kerst	Hayden Carruth	James Branch Cabell
Friedrich Nietzsche	Helent Hunt Jackson	James DeMille
Fyodor Dostoyevsky	Helen Nicolay	James Joyce
G.A. Henty	Hendrik Conscience	James Lane Allen
G.K. Chesterton	Hendy David Thoreau	James Lane Allen
Gabrielle E. Jackson	Henri Barbusse	James Oliver Curwood
Garrett P. Serviss	Henrik Ibsen	James Oppenheim
Gaston Leroux	Henry Adams	James Otis
George A. Warren	Henry Ford	James R. Driscoll
George Ade	Henry Frost	Jane Abbott
Geroge Bernard Shaw	Henry James	Jane Austen
George Cary Eggleston	Henry Jones Ford	Jane L. Stewart
George Durston	Henry Seton Merriman	Janet Aldridge
George Ebers	Henry W Longfellow	Jens Peter Jacobsen
George Eliot	Herbert A. Giles	Jerome K. Jerome
George Gissing	Herbert Carter	Jessie Graham Flower
George MacDonald	Herbert N. Casson	John Buchan
George Meredith	Herman Hesse	John Burroughs
George Orwell	Hildegard G. Frey	John Cournos
George Sylvester Viereck	Homer	John F. Kennedy
George Tucker	Honore De Balzac	John Gay
George W. Cable	Horace B. Day	John Glasworthy
George Wharton James	Horace Walpole	John Habberton
Gertrude Atherton	Horatio Alger Jr.	John Joy Bell
Gordon Casserly	Howard Pyle	John Kendrick Bangs
Grace E. King	Howard R. Garis	John Milton
Grace Gallatin	Hugh Lofting	John Philip Sousa
Grace Greenwood	Hugh Walpole	John Taintor Foote
Grant Allen	Humphry Ward	Jonas Lauritz Idemil Lie
Guillermo A. Sherwell	Ian Maclaren	Jonathan Swift
Gulielma Zollinger	Inez Haynes Gillmore	Joseph A. Altsheler
Gustav Flaubert	Irving Bacheller	Joseph Carey
H. A. Cody	Isabel Cecilia Williams	Joseph Conrad
H. B. Irving	Isabel Hornibrook	Joseph E. Badger Jr
H.C. Bailey	Israel Abrahams	Joseph Hergesheimer
H. G. Wells	Ivan Turgenev	Joseph Jacobs
H. H. Munro	J.G.Austin	Jules Vernes
H. Irving Hancock	J. Henri Fabre	Julian Hawthrone
H. R. Naylor	J. M. Barrie	Julie A Lippmann
H. Rider Haggard	J. M. Walsh	Justin Huntly McCarthy
H. W. C. Davis	J. Macdonald Oxley	Kakuzo Okakura
Haldeman Julius	J. R. Miller	Karle Wilson Baker
Hall Caine	J. S. Fletcher	Kate Chopin
Hamilton Wright Mabie	J. S. Knowles	Kenneth Grahame
Hans Christian Andersen	J. Storer Clouston	Kenneth McGaffey
Harold Avery	J. W. Duffield	Kate Langley Bosher
Harold McGrath	Jack London	Kate Langley Bosher
Harriet Beecher Stowe	Jacob Abbott	Katherine Cecil Thurston
Harry Castlemon	James Allen	Katherine Stokes
Harry Coghill	James Andrews	L. A. Abbot
Harry Houidini	James Baldwin	L. T. Meade

L. Frank Baum
Latta Griswold
Laura Dent Crane
Laura Lee Hope
Laurence Housman
Lawrence Beasley
Leo Tolstoy
Leonid Andreyev
Lewis Carroll
Lewis Sperry Chafer
Lilian Bell
Lloyd Osbourne
Louis Hughes
Louis Joseph Vance
Louis Tracy
Louisa May Alcott
Lucy Fitch Perkins
Lucy Maud Montgomery
Luther Benson
Lydia Miller Middleton
Lyndon Orr
M. Corvus
M. H. Adams
Margaret E. Sangster
Margret Howth
Margaret Vandercook
Margaret W. Hungerford
Margret Penrose
Maria Edgeworth
Maria Thompson Daviess
Mariano Azuela
Marion Polk Angellotti
Mark Overton
Mark Twain
Mary Austin
Mary Catherine Crowley
Mary Cole
Mary Hastings Bradley
Mary Roberts Rinehart
Mary Rowlandson
M. Wollstonecraft Shelley
Maud Lindsay
Max Beerbohm
Myra Kelly
Nathaniel Hawthrone
Nicolo Machiavelli
O. F. Walton
Oscar Wilde

Owen Johnson
P.G. Wodehouse
Paul and Mabel Thorne
Paul G. Tomlinson
Paul Severing
Percy Brebner
Percy Keese Fitzhugh
Peter B. Kyne
Plato
Quincy Allen
R. Derby Holmes
R. L. Stevenson
R. S. Ball
Rabindranath Tagore
Rahul Alvares
Ralph Bonehill
Ralph Henry Barbour
Ralph Victor
Ralph Waldo Emmerson
Rene Descartes
Ray Cummings
Rex Beach
Rex E. Beach
Richard Harding Davis
Richard Jefferies
Richard Le Gallienne
Robert Barr
Robert Frost
Robert Gordon Anderson
Robert L. Drake
Robert Lansing
Robert Lynd
Robert Michael Ballantyne
Robert W. Chambers
Rosa Nouchette Carey
Rudyard Kipling
Saint Augustine
Samuel B. Allison
Samuel Hopkins Adams
Sarah Bernhardt
Sarah C. Hallowell
Selma Lagerlof
Sherwood Anderson
Sigmund Freud
Standish O'Grady
Stanley Weyman
Stella Benson
Stella M. Francis

Stephen Crane
Stewart Edward White
Stijn Streuvels
Swami Abhedananda
Swami Parmananda
T. S. Ackland
T. S. Arthur
The Princess Der Ling
Thomas A. Janvier
Thomas A Kempis
Thomas Anderton
Thomas Bailey Aldrich
Thomas Bulfinch
Thomas De Quincey
Thomas Dixon
Thomas H. Huxley
Thomas Hardy
Thomas More
Thornton W. Burgess
U. S. Grant
Upton Sinclair
Valentine Williams
Various Authors
Vaughan Kester
Victor Appleton
Victor G. Durham
Victoria Cross
Virginia Woolf
Wadsworth Camp
Walter Camp
Walter Scott
Washington Irving
Wilbur Lawton
Wilkie Collins
Willa Cather
Willard F. Baker
William Dean Howells
William le Queux
W. Makepeace Thackeray
William W. Walter
William Shakespeare
Winston Churchill
Yei Theodora Ozaki
Yogi Ramacharaka
Young E. Allison
Zane Grey